All of this, and much [...] itself part of the cha[...] people to discover t[...] Car ownership in Ty[...] lowest in the country [...] option of driving. Car owners can also choose to leave the vehicle at home for a change.

The benefits of walking, and of maintaining an inquisitive mind, are well proven in terms of physical and mental health. And in Peter Donaghy and John Laidler, who are well experienced in the field of compiling interest-packed walks, we have the very best of guides. Off you go!

Tony Henderson

Environment Editor of *The Journal* newspaper and author of the hardback book *My Country: Discovering North East England*, which highlights the region's special places

Acknowledgements

The authors would like to thank Mike Parker and his staff at Nexus, including especially David De Ivey and Helen Fox, for their encouragement and invaluable assistance in bringing this project to fruition. At the same time we are also grateful to the many "volunteers" among our friends who have shared their experiences of these walks with us and who have offered many helpful comments. Finally we would like to thank our wives, Jeanne and Gillian, for their enthusiastic support and, not least, for completing every walk at least twice!

INTRODUCTION

This book brings together thirty-six walks published in 2003, in the form of six separate booklets, together with fourteen new walks all accessible from the Tyne and Wear Metro network. The original walks have been amended, where necessary, to take into account changes that have occurred as a result of the diversion of paths and the constant development of building works. The new walks serve to enlarge the scope and diversity of the original series and to take into consideration the opening of the new station at Northumberland Park. The arrangement of the fifty in sequence, as far as possible, enables users to link and extend walks if desired.

All the walks start and end at a Metro Station, usually, but not always, at a different station, and not, of course, by the shortest possible route! See the index at the end of this book together with the Metro map on the back cover for the location of the starting points for all the walks. The ideal Metro ticket for these walks is a DaySaver as this gives you all day unlimited travel on the whole Metro system.

These walks provide an opportunity to obtain insights into a wide variety of the cultural and historical attractions of the region. They encompass both rural and urban environments. At the same time they offer people of different age and abilities the chance to take some healthy exercise in parts of the North-East they might never have considered. Users will find delightful green rural spaces at the end of the Metro lines and also many surprising green corridors within the urban areas. They will also be encouraged to explore interesting and unusual parts of Gateshead, Newcastle, North and South Shields, and Sunderland.

Each description is preceded by an outline of the route with guidance regarding the nature of the terrain and the availability of refreshments. One of the joys of such walks is taking a well-earned rest at a conveniently placed café or pub! However, references to cafes and pubs do not necessarily imply recommendation and, as with places of interest, readers need to be aware of different opening and closing times.

Detailed maps are not required in order to complete these walks, however, a simple diagram provides an idea of the direction and shape of each walk. In the main, these are all-weather walks on the level along pavements and surfaced footpaths and hence accessible all the year round for all the family without specialist equipment. Nevertheless, occasionally a route may lead across a field that can be muddy, there may be stiles to surmount, a steep incline or steps to climb. It is therefore advisable to check the description before deciding upon the suitability of each walk for a particular occasion.

Every attempt has been made to ensure that all the instructions are correct at the time of publication. However, it is inevitable, that changes will occur – road and construction work may lead to paths being diverted, livestock may be introduced into fields, stiles, signs and gates may disappear and pubs may even have a change of name!

And just a word about respect. Do be careful to respect yourself by ensuring that you are properly clothed and shod for the conditions you may encounter; and do respect the environment in which you are walking by following the country code and observing relevant signs.

Finally, we hope you will enjoy all that is to be found within such easy reach of the Tyne and Wear Metro network.

Peter Donaghy and John Laidler are retired university lecturers, experienced walkers and co-authors of Lakeland Church Walks (2001) and Northumbria Church Walks (2002) (published by Sigma Leisure).

THE WALKS

Stations between Airport and Central Station

Stations between South Hylton and Fellgate

ROUTE - From the Airport to Ponteland and through a pleasant park and some delightful countryside to Dissington Bridge. Then return via the impressive Darras Hall Estate

TERRAIN - Mainly on the level. After an initial section on pavements, the route is mostly on field paths, farm tracks and a dismantled railway

REFRESHMENTS - A pub and a restaurant on the way to Ponteland and a wide range of possibilities in Ponteland

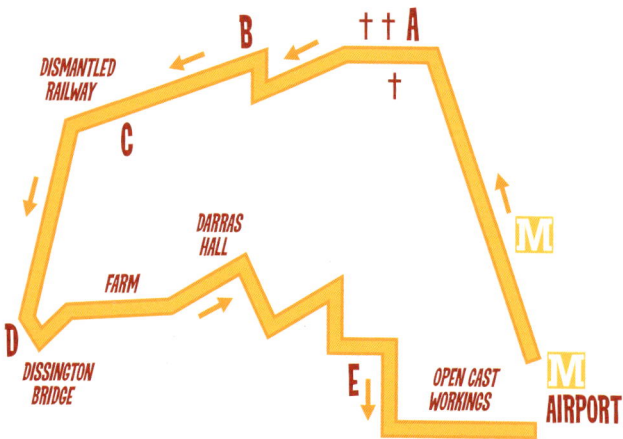

Leave Airport Metro Station and follow the signs into the Airport Terminal. Go out from the terminal building by the first exit, a few yards ahead on the left. Turn left and follow the pavement towards the airport exit. Just after the roundabout, cross to the other side of the road and go onto the path ahead of you. Follow the path until you reach a roundabout. Continue ahead and pass Stone Cottage and Stonehaven Lodge bed and breakfast on your right. Carry on past The Badger pub and the entrance to Dobbies Garden Centre and Restaurant. Continue ahead for just over ¾ of a mile until you reach the Diamond Inn opposite Ponteland Methodist Church. Walk ahead a few yards and turn left to cross over at the pedestrian lights. **A**

Turn right and walk ahead. Over to the right you pass the ancient church of St Mary the Virgin and the Vicar's Pele

Tower (c1400), a plaque behind the metal gate gives interesting historical information. You pass a sign to the Merton Way shopping centre, which has a variety of shops and cafes. Just before St Matthew's Roman Catholic Church (1947 and later extensions) on your right, turn left into Ponteland Park. Follow the path for about 50 yards then turn right and proceed along the narrow path with the River Pont over to your left. Cross the bridge. Bear right, then take the right-hand fork and walk ahead to cross the Ponteland Park Millennium Bridge. At a T-junction of paths, turn right. After about 30 yards, at a junction of paths, turn right to exit the park onto a narrow road (Fox Covert Lane). Turn right and walk to a junction with a main road. Turn left and walk along The Beeches for about 50 yards. Turn left onto the public footpath to Dissington Bridge. (The entrance to the path is down the driveway, tucked in near the garden of the house). **B**

Follow the grassy path to reach a stile, with a farm (West Houses) over to the right. Cross the stile. Walk straight ahead, with hedges on your left, along the field boundaries via a series of stiles. At the corner of a large field, turn right to continue round the perimeter, with the hedge still on your left, to a gateway and a waymarked stile on your left. Turn left and walk ahead, with the hedge on your right. At the end of the field, bear left and walk 50 yards to a ladder stile. Cross the stile and walk straight ahead towards a barn. Cross another ladder stile. Walk past the barn. Bear slightly right to walk diagonally across the field, aiming for the last house on the right of the line of houses seen through the trees and bushes ahead. You arrive at a waymarked ladder stile. Go over the stile and proceed ahead with the hedgerow on your left. Ignore the ladder stile on your left and continue skirting the edge of Darras Hall Estate. After the last house, cross a ladder stile and walk along the field boundary into a wood. Proceed ahead between the trees to a field. Walk ahead, with the hedge on your left. At the end of the field go up steps at the right-hand side of the bridge to the dismantled railway. Turn left and walk for 15 yards, then turn right to descend to some steps into a field. Proceed ahead, cross a ladder stile and follow the path to a waymarked ladder stile. **C**

Cross the stile. Bear right and walk ahead. Where the wire fence on your right makes a right-angle turn, bear right and proceed ahead, now with the River Pont on your left. Cross a little plank bridge and shortly go over a waymarked footbridge. Walk ahead, with the stream on your left, past a footbridge. Follow the path as it bears right, with trees over to your left, to a ladder stile. Go over the stile and bear left, to proceed around the field edge, with the hedgerow on your left, to arrive at a stile near a gate. Cross the stile, bear slightly right and walk towards the bushes and the banks of a river ahead. Turn right and follow the path, which runs roughly parallel to the River Pont on your left, to the end of the field to cross a stile. Continue in the same direction. Follow the path up steps and emerge onto a minor road at Dissington Bridge. **D**

Turn left and proceed along the road for about 350 yards. Just before the Medburn sign take the public bridleway on the left for "Darras Hall 1, Ponteland 2¾". Follow the perimeter of the field and then the broad track that climbs to the entrance to a farm (Donkins House). You are recommended to follow the alternative path round the farm area. Continue along the broad farm track which leads into a narrow road (The Crescent). Walk ahead to the road junction and turn right. Walk for a hundred yards or so then take the public bridleway "Ponteland 1¾" on the left. Keep to the main path, which follows the line of a dismantled railway, until it reaches a road. Cross the road (Broadway). Continue ahead, with the modern Ponteland United Reformed Church on your right, to pass some pleasant housing before rejoining the disused railway track. Continue to the next road. Turn right and walk along the road (Eastern Way) to a crossroads. Turn left and proceed to the roundabout ahead. Turn right, in the direction "Newcastle, Throckley", and walk to the next roundabout. Turn left, in the direction "Newcastle, Airport". Cross the road with care near the "Rotary Way" sign and proceed ahead on the wide grass verge to a fingerpost "Hold House ½" on your right. **E**

Go over the stile and walk ahead on the broad farm track. After half a mile, at a crossing of paths, turn left onto the public footpath to the Airport. Keep on the path which passes a small pond on your right. Where the path turns left, go over the waymarked stile ahead and walk towards the Airport buildings. You walk on a narrow path between wire fences until you reach a vehicular track near the former opencast workings. Bear right and walk along the broad track. Where the track turns left you leave it to go right, through a gap in the fence. Bear left and follow the faint path for about 30 yards to come to a field. Bear left to walk along the field boundary, with the hedge on your left. Turn left when you reach a large metal gate on your left.

Walk along the broad surfaced track. At a fingerpost (which gives directions for the way you have just come), turn left and follow the pavement to the busy dual carriageway. Cross both lanes with care and make your way back to the Airport Terminal, Airport Metro Station and the end of the walk.

ROUTE – To High Callerton, then through the pleasant Darras Hall Estate, before returning directly to the airport

TERRAIN – On the level, mainly on field paths (some of which can be muddy), metalled paths and pavements. There is one section on a quiet estate road

REFRESHMENTS – At the Airport

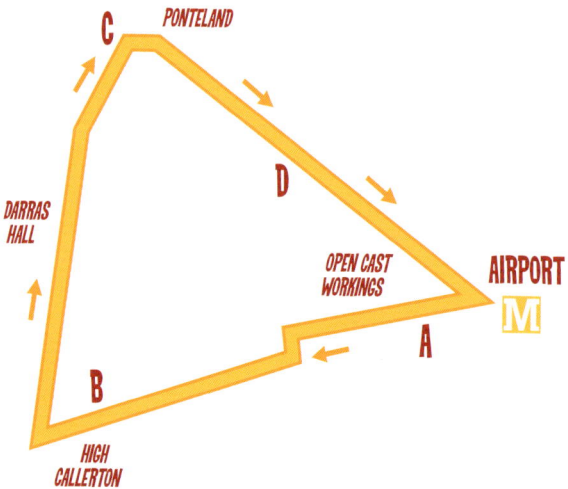

Leave Airport Metro Station and follow the signs into the Airport Terminal. Go out from the terminal building by the first exit door, a few yards ahead on the left. When you are outside the building, turn left and follow the pavement towards the airport exit. Just after the roundabout, turn right to cross the road and walk ahead for 30 yards. Now turn left and walk ahead to cross the minor road and pick up the pavement. Follow the pavement as it bears right to come to a crossing point. With extreme care, cross both lanes of the dual carriageway. Turn left and follow the path to a fingerpost "Black Callerton 1 1/4 miles, High Callerton 1 1/2 miles". Walk in the direction indicated up the broad track to arrive at a large metal gate. Immediately after the gate, turn right to walk ahead along the field boundary, with the hedgerow on your right. At the field corner bear left and walk for 20 yards.

Then turn right and walk for 40 yards, initially straight ahead, then following the faint path as it bears to the right to reach the field corner and a gap in the wire fence. Go through the gap. You are now near a former area of open cast mining; a warning sign for walkers "Caution site traffic" indicates that you need to take care here. **A**

Turn left and walk along the wide vehicular track. You can see the opencast workings over to your right. When the track bears to the right (near a warning sign for the operator 's drivers "caution footpath crossing"), walk straight ahead to join a narrow path running between two wire fences. Proceed along the path for a few hundred yards and cross a waymarked stile. Continue in the same direction, now on a broad farm track. Keep on the track as it skirts a pond on the left. Follow the track as it takes a 90 degree turn to the right and walk 300 yards to a set of fingerposts at a crossing of paths. Go straight ahead on the farm track in the direction "High Callerton". You pass a property (Hold House) on your left. Continue on to a small settlement (High Callerton) on your left. At the end of the farm track, exit onto a road. **B**

Cross the road and go into Edge Hill. Walk ahead and, after 200 yards or so, turn into the road on the right, which a faint sign identifies as Eastern Way. You are now walking through part of Darras Hall Estate with its wide variety of residential properties and large gardens. The walk continues along Eastern Way for just under a mile. After about three quarters of a mile you cross a main road. Continue ahead for a few hundred yards until, shortly after Meadow Court, you arrive at metal barriers on your right. Turn right, onto the path. This is a dismantled railway which runs between the gardens of Darras Hall houses. Keep on the path for just under half a mile until you reach another set of metal barriers **C**. Go through the barriers and turn right. (If you wish to visit Ponteland, you can continue straight ahead to arrive at the Ponteland Memorial Hall).

Walk along the narrow path on the edge of the green area. After 70 yards or so, at a crossing of paths, turn right onto the metalled path, which is another dismantled railway track. Carry on and exit onto a road. Cross the road and go onto the continuation of the path. After 50 yards, where the path divides, take the right-hand fork. Carry straight on, passing Ponteland High School over to your right. Continue until the path meets a road. **D**

Cross the busy road with care and go onto the continuation of the path. Proceed along the path, ignoring paths to the left and right. You pass a newly-planted area, with supports and protective tubes, on your right. Carry on until, just beyond two boulders, you arrive at a service road. Cross the road and go through the waymarked gateway on the right. Walk ahead a short distance to emerge at a wide track. Turn left and walk past the metal gates on your left to arrive at a pavement near a roundabout. Now retrace your steps to the terminal, Airport Metro Station and the end of the walk.

ROUTE - Starts on a secondary road from the airport and detours via a nature reserve to Woolsington. Then follows a track to Newbiggin Hall en route for Bank Foot

TERRAIN - Mostly on the level, with one long gradual gentle ascent. The beginning and end of the walk is mainly on pavements but the middle section is on tracks, which can be muddy

REFRESHMENTS - Facilities at the airport, a pub/restaurant and a tea room en route and a pub near Bank Foot Metro Station

Leave Airport Metro Station and follow the signs into the Airport Terminal. Go out from the terminal building by the first exit door, a few yards ahead on the left. When you are outside the building, turn left and follow the pavement towards the airport exit. At the roundabout, turn left onto the metalled footpath and proceed ahead. You pass the Premier Travel Inn and terraces of cottages on your right. The airport is on your left and your journey on the next half mile or so might well be punctuated by the sight and sound of aeroplanes taking off and landing. You pass a road on your left to the freight village, another part of the airport's domain. Just opposite The Wheatsheaf, turn left onto the metalled footpath. **A**

Follow the path. At a junction, just after crossing a small footbridge, turn right and proceed ahead to arrive at a road. Groundstar House is ahead. Cross the road, turn left and walk to a small yellow-brick building. Immediately after this building turn right and follow a stony path for a few yards to join another road. Turn right and proceed to a junction. Cross the road and join the grassy track. Keep on the path which leads to an information panel which describes Abbotswood, part of Newcastle Airport Landscape and Wildlife Strategy, where the amount of woodland is being increased by the planting of new trees. Cross the road and continue in the same direction. Follow the path as it wends its way through woodland and an open area to come to an information panel giving details of Abbotswood South. Exit through a kissing gate onto a metalled path. Turn right and walk a short distance to join a pavement. Turn left and walk for about two hundred yards to a mini roundabout. Cross the road with care and go into The Oval. Walk ahead then turn left and proceed along Woolsington Gardens to its junction with Green Lane. (Refreshments are available at Sandra's Village Tea Rooms, a few yards along to your left). **B**

Turn right and walk ahead. You pass a sign "Public Bridleway Low Newbiggin ⅔". Follow the public bridleway (called Black Lane), which comes to the Metro line. Cross the line, carefully observing the instructions. Continue on the bridleway, which goes on a bridge over the Newcastle-Airport road. Keep to the main path which soon starts a gradual ascent. At a definite division of paths, keep straight ahead and carry on climbing gradually to come to a junction with a metalled path. Turn left and follow the path, with hedgerows on both sides, to where it meets a road. **C**

Continue ahead to a T- junction. Turn left and walk ahead. At a convenient point, cross over to the pavement on the opposite side. Walk ahead passing a roundabout and going over a bridge over the dual carriageway. After passing another roundabout, proceed ahead to Bank Foot Metro Station and the end of the walk. The Twin Farms pub is a short distance beyond the station.

ROUTE - Through Coxlodge, Gosforth and along the Nuns Moor to Kenton, passing a wide variety of housing, a small nature reserve and a reclaimed quarry

TERRAIN - Mainly on the level along pavements and surfaced paths with one section on grassland. There is one longish gentle ascent

REFRESHMENTS - Two pubs on route and a café at Tesco at Kingston Park

M KINGSTON PARK

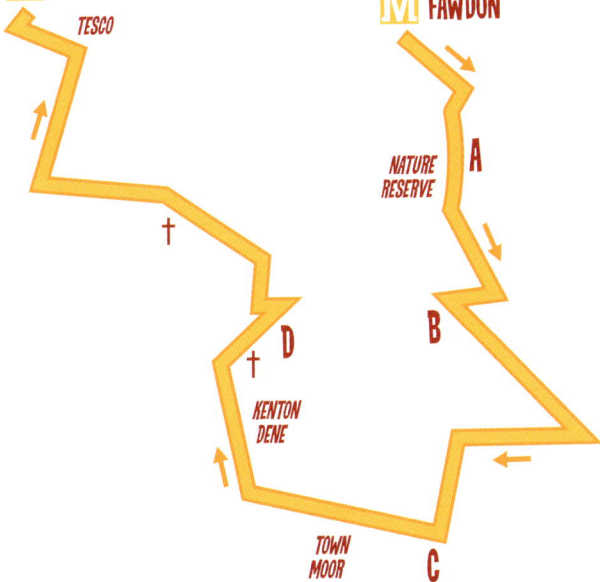

TESCO

M FAWDON

NATURE RESERVE

A

B

KENTON DENE

D

TOWN MOOR

C

Leave Fawdon Metro Station: from Platform 1, walk down the pavement, turn right and cross the level crossing; from Platform 2, turn left. Walk up The Meadows. (If starting out from Platform 2, when convenient cross to the other side of The Meadows). At the crossroads just beyond The Jubilee pub, go straight across, turn right and walk a few yards, then turn left. Walk ahead, past Leagreen Court Bungalows, and turn left into Coxlodge Road. Proceed ahead, then turn right to walk to the end of Mary Agnes Street. Turn left and walk a short distance, then go through the ornamental entrance on the right into a nature reserve. **A**

Turn immediately right and follow the path round to the Northumberland Wildlife Trust Activity Centre on your left. Just past the centre, bear right and walk ahead to join a road near the clock tower. You are now in the centre of what was the huge complex of the former Coxlodge Asylum, opened in 1868. Later extensions included the construction of the clock tower block in 1900. The hospital is considerably smaller now; many of the older buildings have been converted into apartments and there is a great deal of modern housing and some light industrial development. Turn right and proceed ahead. Where the road ends continue on the path to cross another road and keep in the same direction to a T-junction. Turn left and follow the road, passing refurbished former hospital buildings on your left. At the next T-junction turn right and walk to the crossroads. Use the traffic lights to cross the road to arrive at the Post Office on the corner of a parade of shops. **B**

If you are in need of refreshment, the Duke of Wellington pub is a few yards up Kenton Lane. To continue the walk, proceed, past the Post Office and Norseman Travel, along the busy road (Kenton Road). Pass the Kenton Park Shopping Centre on your right and carry on to a roundabout. Turn right and walk along Kenton Avenue which has a wide variety of residential properties. At the T-junction turn left and walk ahead, passing Wyndham Primary School on your right. Where the road bears left walk straight ahead, past the Sheldon Grove sign on your right, and go along the alleyway running between the houses to emerge onto the Nuns Moor. **C**

Walk ahead for a few yards, then turn right and follow the path which roughly parallels the moor boundary about 100 yards or so over to the right. When you pass the second tall apartment block continue ahead to the lone bush near the railings. After rain it can be very muddy around here. Turn right and walk alongside the railings to exit onto a footpath. Walk straight ahead to a crossing of paths and continue ahead on the path with seats. You are now in Kenton Dene, a recreational area reclaimed from a quarry and landfill site. There is a gradual ascent until the path levels out and bears right along an avenue of young lime trees. You pass the curved roof of the Church of the Ascension (1956) on your right before descending to exit onto a road. **D**

Turn left and cross the road at the pedestrian lights. Walk along the road ahead (Drayton Road). At the T-junction turn left and go along Balmain Road. At the next T-junction turn left onto Hillsview Avenue. Walk past St Cuthbert's Catholic Church (1960) then immediately turn left to walk along Bromford Road. At the end go straight ahead on the broad paved path. Carry on along Hartburn Walk. Pass Kenton Bar Primary School on your left and continue ahead. At the shops turn right and carry on to exit onto a busy road near a bus shelter. Turn right and follow the road as it gradually descends. Where the road bears right, cross over with care and go straight ahead on the metalled path. You can see Tesco ahead and, beyond in the distance, the new, modern headquarters of Sage plc. At a crossing of paths turn left and walk a short distance to cross a bridge. Continue ahead past Tesco on your right. Just before the Tesco garage turn right to join the entrance/exit road to Tesco. Cross the road with care, turn left and walk ahead. At the second roundabout turn right and proceed to Kingston Park Metro Station and the end of the walk.

Coxlodge Clock Tower

WALK 5

Kingston Park to Callerton Parkway (5.5 miles)

➤ **ROUTE** – Alongside the Metro line to Bankfoot, through a dene and on to Westerhope. Across a golf course and along field paths, to Woolsington. Then via an interesting environmental development to Callerton Parkway

🚶 **TERRAIN** – Mainly on the level, using metalled paths and tracks

☕ **REFRESHMENTS** – There is a tearoom at Woolsington and a pub/restaurant at Callerton Parkway

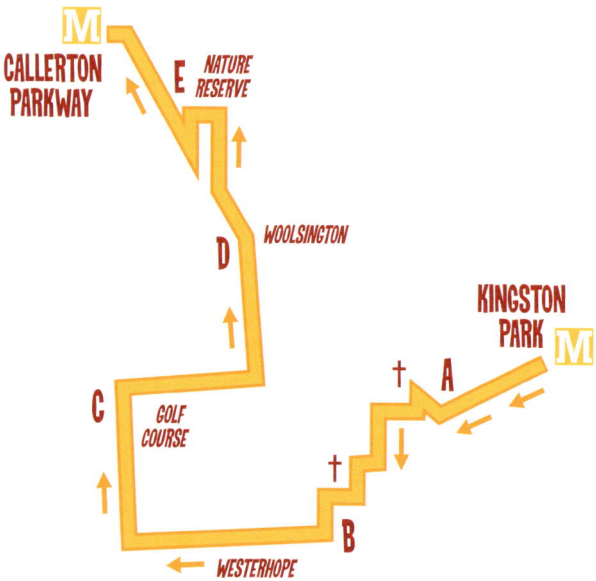

Leave Kingston Park Metro Station: from Platform 1, exit down the ramp, turn right to cross the Metro line, then turn right onto the service road, with the Metro line on your right; from Platform 2, exit down the ramp, cross the road and join the service road. Proceed ahead. At the end of the road, carry on straight ahead along the metalled path. You arrive at a main road. Cross the road with care and continue ahead on the metalled path. Keep on the main path, ignoring paths off to the left. Carry on and go through a subway. At a junction of paths, bear left and shortly, at an intersection of paths, bear left again. Walk through the woodland (Newbiggin Dene). At the end of the dene, bear left and go up the slope. Exit through metal barriers to a road. **A**

Turn right and follow the road (Hedgehope Road) to a T-junction. Over to right is St Wilfrid's Church (1967). Cross the road, turn left, walk a few yards then turn right past the doctor's surgery to the metalled path ahead. Proceed ahead, with the ferocious looking railings on your left. At the intersection of paths turn left, following the line of the railings, and walk ahead. Turn right onto the second path (with streetlights). At the junction, near the music notes sculpture, bear left and carry on between houses to a T-junction. Turn right and proceed along the road (Whittingham Road) to a junction with a busy road. Turn right and walk to the T-junction, with St Mark's Catholic Church (1979) on your right. Cross the main road, with care, using the traffic island on your right, and turn left. Walk ahead to the roundabout. **B**

You are in a large suburb of Newcastle called Westerhope. Originally, it was a small country village, established in the 1890s. The founding families named their settlement to indicate that their move west gave them hope for a better life, away from the crowded garden-less terraces of Newcastle. Turn right and proceed ahead, on the pavement and then a grass verge. (Walkers with pushchairs might prefer to make use of the pavement on the other side of the road). At a crossroads with traffic lights, turn right and walk along the narrow road to arrive near the clubhouse of Westerhope Golf Club. Carry on in the same direction past Whorlton Grange residential home. There is a sign which warns walkers of the danger of flying golf balls. You should respect the etiquette of the game and keep still and quiet if golfers are playing shots nearby. Walk along the tree-lined track and onto the course. Walk ahead with the trees on your right. Bear right past the 150 yards marker post to pick up a track with a metal fence/hedge on your right. Exit from the course via a metal stile. **C**

Turn right and walk along the grassy area with the hedge on your left. If it is wet you may prefer to use the road over to your right. A short distance after passing some tall conifers, turn left into an entrance and immediately right to continue in the same direction along the narrow lane. You come to a track on your left (at this point, on your right, there is a sign for 99-129 Hareydene). Go onto the track and proceed ahead. At a junction of paths continue straight on. Cross the bridge over the dual carriageway. Carry on and cross the Metro line, via the carefully designed safety gates, to arrive in Woolsington village. **D**

Turn left to pass (and possibly visit) Sandra's Village Tea Room. Walk to the traffic island and cross the road. Turn left and proceed ahead, past some interesting properties. After about a quarter of a mile, just before a bus stop, turn right onto the public footpath to Woolsington Hall. After 50 yards an information panel on the left explains that you have arrived at South Abbotswood, part of Newcastle Airport Landscape and Wildlife Strategy. Carry on until the public footpath meets a road with double yellow lines on both sides (Middle Drive). Turn left and walk along the road to a T-junction. Another information panel, on the right, gives details of this part of Abbotswood. **E**

If time permits you can explore the little woodland area. To continue the walk, turn left and walk to the junction with the main road. Turn right and proceed ahead to the junction. Turn left and cross the road with care and walk past The Wheatsheaf pub and restaurant to arrive at Callerton Parkway Metro station and the end of the walk.

Exit Callerton Parkway Metro Station onto a road near a level crossing. Turn left and walk straight ahead, making use of the grass verges. Keep in the same direction, past two roundabouts. After a further 300 yards, just before some cottages, go onto the public bridleway on the right. Walk ahead to reach a waymarked gate on the left. Go through the gate and follow the track as it bears right to reach another waymarked gate. Go through the gate and turn left. Now follow the broad track which soon passes flight path warning lights on your right. You might see (and hear!) an aeroplane coming in to land. The track eventually skirts a pond on the left and you arrive at a gate, next to a wide metal gate. Go through the gate and follow the wide track to exit onto a pavement near a roundabout. Bear left and walk to the end of the pavement and, with extreme care, cross both lanes of the dual carriageway. Turn right and follow the path towards the airport buildings. A few yards before a roundabout, you reach a road and path on your left. Cross the road. **A**

Turn left to follow the path until you reach a roundabout. Keep walking in the same direction and cross the road. Pass Stone Cottage Bed and Breakfast on your right. Carry on past The Badger pub and the entrance to Dobbies Garden Centre and Restaurant. Shortly you come to Ponteland and a 30mph speed restriction sign. About 100 yards past this sign, just before a bungalow, you reach a fingerpost showing "Prestwick ½". **B**

Turn right and walk straight across the field, with the fence on your left. Exit the field by a waymarked gate. Walk straight ahead, then bear left as indicated and exit the farm area by a waymarked kissing gate. The entrance drive to Prestwick Hall is on the left. Turn right and walk to a gateway and bear right to walk a short distance to join a road. Turn left, and making use of pavements and grass verges, walk ahead, past the varied dwellings of Prestwick, to reach The Martins on your right. Just beyond the property, go onto the narrow road on the left. **C**

Proceed along the road, going through open country and possibly hearing the pleasant drone of light aircraft overhead, until eventually you come to a crossroads. Turn left and walk ahead. Where the road bears right to Prestwick Mill Farm, carry straight on. You pass Ponteland Golf Course on your left. At the junction of paths, turn left and keep on the track as it makes its way past a pond on your right to reach farm buildings and cottages in a pretty setting at Eland Hall Farm. Carry on along the road, past a housing estate on the left. Continue, with the River Pont on your right, to come to traffic lights in Ponteland village. **D**

You are now at the point where you head back to the airport. However, before returning you may wish to explore the attractions of the village and possibly stop for refreshments. To complete the walk, turn left past The Smithy Bistro and walk ahead. After about three-quarters of a mile you come to the footpath that took you to Prestwick **B**. Continue straight on to retrace your steps back to **A**.

Cross to the other side of the airport entrance road and follow the pavement to the terminal building. Go into the terminal and turn right. Walk to the Metro sign and follow directions to arrive at the Airport Metro Station and the end of the walk.

Wansbeck Road to Four Lane Ends (5.5 miles)

ROUTE - Through pleasant urban parts of Gosforth and then through more open areas, passing a golf course and an animal sanctuary, before reaching Four Lane Ends

TERRAIN - Almost entirely on the level on pavements and surfaced tracks

REFRESHMENTS - Pub near Wansbeck Metro station and a variety of possibilities on Gosforth High Street and at Four Lane Ends

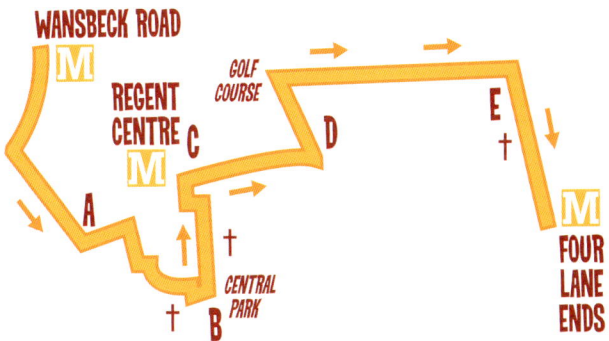

Exit from Wansbeck Road Metro Station, Platform 2, to the main road (Wansbeck Road South), turn left and walk ahead, past The Collingwood pub and a parade of shops, to the traffic lights at Jubilee Road. (If leaving from Platform 1, turn right, walk up the road, cross over at the pedestrian crossing, turn right and continue ahead to the traffic lights).

Turn left and proceed along Jubilee Road. You pass the Welford Centre (Day service for adults with learning disabilities) on your right, and the Fire Station on your left. At the traffic lights, opposite St Nicholas Park, with its collection of offices, services and hospital facilities (note the multilingual sign), you reach Regent Avenue. A

Turn left and walk past the Northern Rock complex and then the Children's Services Entrance of St Oswald's Hospice, until you arrive at the Gift Shop and Visitor Centre at the Adult Services Entrance of St Oswald's. Cross to the opposite side of the road and proceed along Archibald Street. At the T-junction, turn right and walk to the pedestrian crossing. Cross over the road, turn left and in a short distance turn right into Ivy Road. Follow Ivy Road as it curves past some neat terraced houses and eventually meets a main road (Gosforth High Street). On the right, you have just passed Trinity Church, originally opened as a Wesleyan Chapel in 1841, now the reflection of the amalgamation of three local churches (A Methodist-United Reformed Church Local Ecumenical Partnership). Cross over the road at the pedestrian lights, turn right and walk the short distance to the traffic lights at St Nicholas Avenue (unless, first of all, you want to find refreshments in the Shopping Centre or on the High Street). **B**

Turn left and proceed into Gosforth Central Park. Just beyond the gates, on your right, there is a notice board that provides some information about the history of the park. The tall structure beyond the park wall is the indoor coaching facility at South Northumberland Cricket ground. Take the second path on the left and walk through the centre of the park, past the war memorial, to a raised area with seats. Just before the steps, turn right and follow the path left, then right to pass a bowling green on your right and exit onto a road (Church Road). Cross the busy road with care, either at the traffic island or lights on your left, to enter Rothwell Road, directly opposite. On the right is St Charles Church (1911), designed by a Belgian architect, Charles Menart. Continue to the end of the street, passing a variety of tiny gardens and turn left at the T-junction. Walk the short distance to the traffic lights at the main road, the B1318. Turn right, cross over Christon Road and walk about 200 yards to the roundabout. Regent Centre Metro station is on your left (useful if you are weary at this point) and Asda is directly ahead. **C**

Turn right and walk down Hollywood Avenue into Garden Village taking the opportunity to cross over to the other side of the road at a convenient point. After about half a mile, as the road bears right, you reach a bus turning point at Woodlea Gardens. **D**

Turn left and walk along the quiet access road with a green area on your right. After about 200 yards, you cross a bridge over the Ouseburn. Continue ahead on the public bridleway "Heathery Lane ¼ 0.4km". The metalled path climbs very gently before it passes between the fairways of Gosforth Golf Club (known locally as "The Bridlepath"). Turn right at the first junction and continue along the lane, between the hedgerows, to a T-junction at a main road (Salters Lane). Cross over the road with care, using the traffic island on your left to join the surfaced track directly opposite. Continue ahead with the business park premises on your left and housing on your right. After a few hundred yards you pass the animal sanctuary at Benton North Farm on your right. Continue ahead and a few yards before the road, turn right past a metal barrier to walk a short distance to the entrance to the Dog and Cat Shelter and Animal Sanctuary. This is open to visitors and contains an interesting assortment of animals as well as a private board suite!. **E**

To continue on the walk, proceed ahead, passing Saint Peter and Saint Paul Roman Catholic Church (1960) and in about half a mile you reach Four Lane Ends Interchange. Cross over the road at the pedestrian lights to Four Lane Ends Metro Station and the end of the walk (unless you wish to continue ahead to seek refreshments from the shops beyond the lights or the pubs to the left).

Gosforth High Street

ROUTE - Follows the Great North Road to Gosforth Park, then makes its way via Melton Park Estate and between fields and a golf course back to South Gosforth

TERRAIN - Mostly on pavements with about half a mile on a surfaced footpath. There are steps over a railway footbridge and a steep climb to South Gosforth Station but this could be avoided by returning to Regent Centre Station

REFRESHMENTS - In Gosforth Park and at South Gosforth

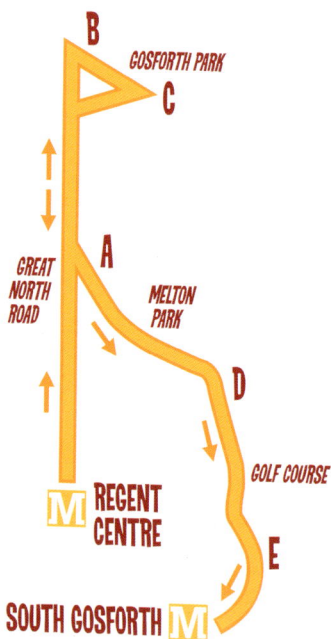

Exit from Regent Centre Metro Station, turn left and follow the pavement beside the main road (Great North Road) for just under 2 miles to Gosforth Park. Initially you walk past Gosforth High School and a parade of shops and then continue, passing the City of Newcastle Golf Club on your left, and The New Three Mile Inn on your right. A few hundred yards after the roundabout at the entrance to Brunton Park, use the pedestrian lights to cross over the road just to the right of Glamis Avenue. **A**

Turn left and with the main road on your left, follow the pavement as it bears right. Through the trees on your right you should be able to obtain glimpses of Newcastle Racecourse which dates from the 1880s when the "Pitman's Derby" now the "Northumberland Plate" was transferred here from the Newcastle Town Moor. Proceed ahead, past the entrances to Gosforth Park with its "Welcome to Newcastle Races" sign and then the Marriott Gosforth Park Hotel. Continue ahead until you reach a road leading to Chandlers Garden Centre. **B**

Turn right and follow the metalled road as it passes the garden centre (with its acquatic centre and its Victorian Tea Rooms) on your right. Continue on the road as it makes its way between the trees until it eventually exits at a junction with a road near the horse-racing stables and the Border Ministrel pub, to the left of which is the 18th century Brandling House (named after its former owners), now incorporated into the grandstand of the racecourse. **C**

Take the opportunity to have refreshments at the pub or at Parklands Golf Club and Driving Centre, a few hundred yards ahead on the left and open to the public. (If time allows, you can enjoy a wander through the park by bearing left through the trees to follow one of several paths to complete a pleasant circuit around the outside of the golf course). However, to continue on the walk, turn right at the road junction and follow the path on the left of the road as it leads out of the park to a road junction just beyond the entrance to the Northumberland Golf Club. Turn left and retrace your steps to Glamis Avenue. **A**

Turn left into the Melton Park housing estate and continue along Glamis Avenue to the junction with Kingsley Ave. Bear left along Kingsley Ave to pass an open green on your right and the stones of an old chapel destroyed in the 17th century. Turn left just before Belmont Ave into Ferndale Ave and at the end of the cul-de-sac go through the waymarked gateway. **D**

Turn right and follow the public footpath "Heathery Lane ⅔". Keep on the broad surfaced track as it makes its way between the trees and the fields and becomes a metalled lane. Continue down the lane, ignoring paths off to the right and left, as it cuts between another golf course (known locally as "The Bridle-path"). The lane crosses a bridge over the River Ouseburn, a tributary of the River Tyne, and eventually arrives at a bus stop and turning circle. **E**

(To avoid the steps over the railway footbridge ahead and the steep climb to South Gosforth Metro Station, you could turn right at this point and follow Hollywood Avenue for just over half a mile to Regent Centre Metro Station).

Now continue ahead for just over 200 yards and when the road bears left to cross the bridge, bear right into Turnberry Way to the footbridge that takes you over the railway line. On the other side of the bridge continue in the same direction down Hunter's Road to a junction of roads at Brandling Villa. Turn right and walk up Station Road (South Gosforth Bank) past the cafes and shops to South Gosforth Metro Station and the end of the walk.

↗ **ROUTE** – From South Gosforth into Jesmond Dene, then through some interesting parts of Jesmond, including a visit to an ancient place of pilgrimage

🚶 **TERRAIN** – On pavements and paths, which can be muddy. There is some undulation and some short flights of steps; one flight is uneven but can be avoided

☕ **REFRESHMENTS** – In South Gosforth and, towards the end of the walk, in Jesmond

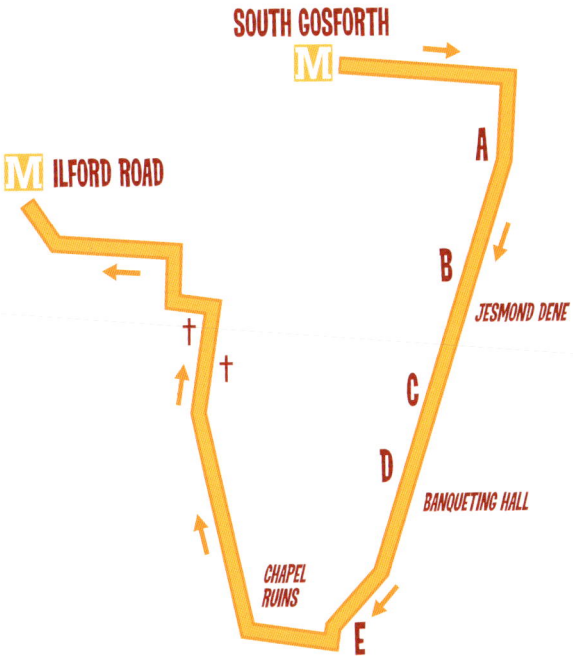

SOUTH GOSFORTH
Ⓜ

A

B

JESMOND DENE

C

D

BANQUETING HALL

Ⓜ **ILFORD ROAD**

†

†

CHAPEL RUINS

E

Leave South Gosforth Metro Station and join a main road. Turn right and follow the road which, shortly, descends past shops and cafes to reach the Brandling Villa pub. Turn right and walk a few yards to traffic lights. Cross at the lights and turn left to follow the pavement as it curves right, over the Ouseburn. It is thought that "Gosforth" means "the ford over the Gos or Ose" - former names of the river. Proceed up Freeman Road. After 200 yards, opposite Lilburn Gardens, go onto the path on the right at the fingerpost "River Tyne 3 ⅓ miles". **A**

Keep on the main path which gradually descends and then levels out. Walk past a footbridge and carry on, with the Ouseburn on your right. Continue as the path ascends, via a short flight of broad steps, to come to a tunnel. Go through the tunnel to emerge into Jesmond Dene. **B**

Much of this area was given for the benefit of the citizens of Newcastle in 1883 by Lord Armstrong (1810 - 1900), the noted industrialist and benefactor. Its densely-wooded, steep banks and many paths make this a popular place for a stroll by local people. Continue ahead on the metalled path, passing steps on your right. After a further 30 yards, turn sharp right and descend the slope to come to the Ouseburn. Turn left and walk along the path with the river on your right. Keep on in the same direction, passing the entrance to a tunnel and North Lodge on your left. At a crossing of paths, bear right, walk ahead and go down the short flight of steps. On your left are the ruins of a mill - a plaque gives details of its history. **C**

(To avoid the uneven steps on the next section, turn right and cross the bridge below the waterfall. Turn left and walk ahead. Go past one bridge and carry on to reach another bridge. Cross this bridge to rejoin the walk at. **D**

To continue the walk from **C**, go down the steps, and take care - they can be slippery. Walk ahead to the second bridge on your right. **D**

The walk continues with the river on your right passing a fingerpost indicating "River Tyne 2½ miles". You come to the entrance to the Fisherman's Lodge restaurant on your left. Go through the gap in the fence on your left, turn right and walk ahead for about 200 yards. Just past a wooden bench on your left, bear right to cross a bridge. Follow the path which brings you to the partly-ruined Banqueting Hall, built for Lord Armstrong. Bear right, walk a short distance then go up the steps on your left and walk to the Hall's main entrance, where a plaque outlines its history. **E**

Cross the road (Jesmond Dene Road) and turn left. Cross Glastonbury Grove and pass the entrance to Ashbourne. Almost immediately, go through the gate on your right. Walk up the path to the lovingly-maintained ruins of the 12th - century St Mary's Chapel, a medieval place of pilgrimage. A plaque gives historical details. Exit the grounds by the gate beyond the chapel. Turn right and go up the road (Reid Park

Road). At the T-junction with a main road (Osborne Road), turn right and proceed ahead. You pass St George's Church (1888), paid for by Charles Mitchell, Lord Armstrong's business partner. Where Osborne Road bears to the left, go straight ahead along North Jesmond Avenue. The Holy Name Roman Catholic Church (1901) is on the left. At the end of the road is the entrance to La Sagesse Convent and School. The school occupies the 19th-century former Jesmond Towers, acquired in 1870 by Charles Mitchell. Turn left and proceed to the end of the school grounds. Turn right and go along the alley to a main road (A189). Turn left and proceed to the pedestrian lights. Cross the road and turn left to walk to Ilford Road Metro Station and the end of the walk.

ROUTE – Follows the Ouseburn to the River Tyne through the delightful Jesmond Dene. Then goes along the buzzing Quayside and on to Central Station

TERRAIN – Mainly on the level along riverside paths. There are two steep climbs, one towards the end of the walk

REFRESHMENTS – An hotel, a coffee shop in Jesmond Dene, three pubs en-route and plenty of possibilities on the Quayside and in Newcastle

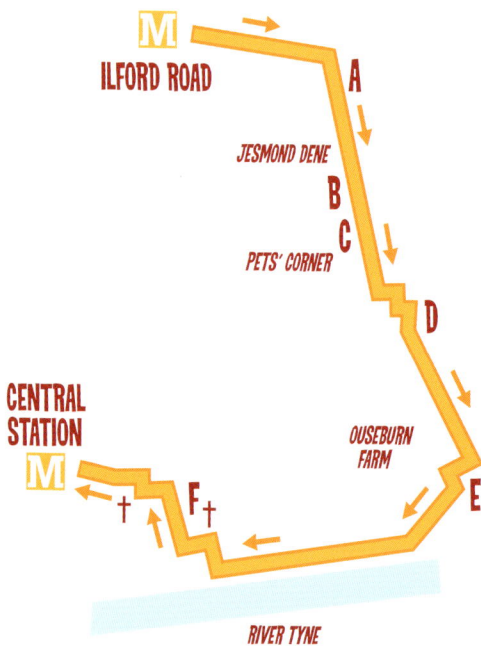

Leave Ilford Road Metro Station: from Platform 1, turn right and walk to the road junction; from Platform 2, turn left and walk to the road junction. Turn left and walk to the traffic lights and cross over the main road. Turn left and walk ahead to where the main road (A189) bears to the left, carry straight on and proceed along the road (Jesmond Dene Road).

On your left you see the Jesmond Dene House hotel, formerly the home of Sir Andrew Noble, one of Lord Armstrong's collaborators. Ignore the "no vehicular access" path. A little further on, cross the road with care to the North West Lodge entrance to Jesmond Dene. **A**

Enter the Dene and follow the metalled path past a covered seating area to a junction just before the Ouseburn, turn right and walk by the side of the river to a bridge. Cross over the bridge. Turn right and proceed ahead with the Ouseburn on your right. The walk continues alongside the river past a fingerpost indicating "River Tyne 2½ miles". You arrive at the entrance to the Fisherman's Lodge restaurant. **B**

A little further on you come to Pets' Corner, The Millfield Coffee Shop and the Jesmond Dene Visitor Centre, which is open on Saturday and Sunday afternoons. A plaque commemorates Lord Armstrong's gift of Jesmond Dene to the citizens of Newcastle in 1883. **C**

Continue in the same direction to go under the metal Armstrong Bridge, where an arts and craft market is held every Sunday. Go under the road bridge and continue in the same direction, Armstrong Park is on the left. At a junction, with three fingerposts, carry straight on. Just after a collection of fingerposts you reach a bridge. Cross the bridge and turn left to pass, on your right the Blue Bell pub and 41 Jesmond Vale, headquarters of Newcastle's Arts Development Team and Schools' Music Service. Go onto the path on your left, near the sign "Ouseburn Park" and walk ahead with the river on your left. Where the river disappears into a culvert, go straight ahead up the steep path. At the junction of paths, turn left and walk to the exit of the park to emerge at a road. Turn right and walk the short distance to the end of the road (Stratford Grove West). Turn left and proceed to the traffic lights. Turn right to cross to the island and then cross over the main road to arrive at an information board. This gives details of the construction of the Ouseburn Culvert in 1907. **D**

Turn right and walk the short distance to take the path on the left. At the junction of paths, turn right and proceed for 20 yards, then take the narrow path on the left. Continue along-side the sports field on your left. This is the site of the running track of the former, short-lived Newcastle Stadium. After about 75 yards the path joins another path. Bear left and after a further 175 yards the path divides. Take the right-hand fork. Keep on this path as it descends towards the arches of the railway bridge. About 20 yards before the end of the path, turn left and follow the path down to go under the railway bridge. Cross a bridge where the Ouseburn emerges from its culvert. Then go under the sweep of the concrete Metro Bridge. After 40 yards the path divides. This area is being transformed by the Ouseburn Farm regeneration project. Refreshments are available at the Ship Inn and The Cluny over to your right.

Take the left-hand fork and walk to a road. Bear right to join the riverside path. Shortly, you pass an area where small pleasure craft are moored. Go underneath a bridge and turn left to go up some steps. At the top of the steps, turn left and walk a few yards to a sign for "Ouseburn Valley, Victoria Tunnel, Quayside" then turn left into Ouse Street. Walk ahead. On the right-hand side, in a little clearing, is an entrance to the Victoria Tunnel. A couple of information boards give details of the tunnel's fascinating history. At the end of Ouse Street, cross over the road with care to the bust of William Lisle Blenkinsopp Coulson. **E**

Over to the left is the confluence of the Ouseburn with the Tyne; usually, some pleasure boats are moored there. Turn right to walk down Horatio Street. The building at the top of the street is the former Sailors' Bethel - a plaque gives detail of its history. At the bottom of the bank turn left onto the Quayside. Turn right and proceed ahead. The last few years have seen a great deal of renovation and revitalisation of this part of the city. The Tyne bridges are ahead and on the opposite bank is the Baltic Centre for Contemporary Art, formerly a 1950's grain warehouse, and a little further on the Sage Music Centre. You pass a number of modern sculptures. Continue ahead towards the Tyne Bridge. A market is held in this part of the Quayside every Sunday morning. On the opposite bank, the Tuxedo Princess nightclub is moored. About 75 yards before the bridge look for the direction sign for All Saints Church. Turn right and proceed along the street (King Street) towards the church. At the junction turn left to go along Queen Street to another junction. Bear right and walk underneath the bridge. Carry on under the railway arch. **F**

The building at the corner opposite is Milburn House (1905), said to be modelled on a ship. Continue ahead up the steep street (Dean Street). When you reach Low Bridge steps on your right, you need to cross Dean Street to the steps opposite. (If the road is busy you can cross at the traffic lights a little further ahead). Go up the steps. At the top, to your left, is a bust of Thomas Bewick (1783 - 1828), the naturalist, painter and wood engraver, who had a workshop here. Turn right and follow the lane to arrive at a statue of Queen Victoria on your right and the north entrance to the Cathedral Church of St Nicholas on your left. The present building dates back, mainly, to the 14th and 15th centuries. Formerly, one of the largest parish churches in the country, it became a cathedral on the creation of the Diocese of Newcastle in 1882. Proceed ahead at the traffic lights and walk along Collingwood Street (of Blaydon Races fame). A short distance ahead is the station clock, Central Station Metro and the end of the walk.

ROUTE – Follows a disused railway between hedgerows, a quiet country lane and a climb through woods to the splendid vantage point of Penshaw Monument

TERRAIN – The disused railway can be muddy in parts. The lane ascends steeply in parts. There is also a steep climb to Penshaw Monument on a footpath and stiles to cross, all of which could be omitted

REFRESHMENTS – Pubs at South Hylton

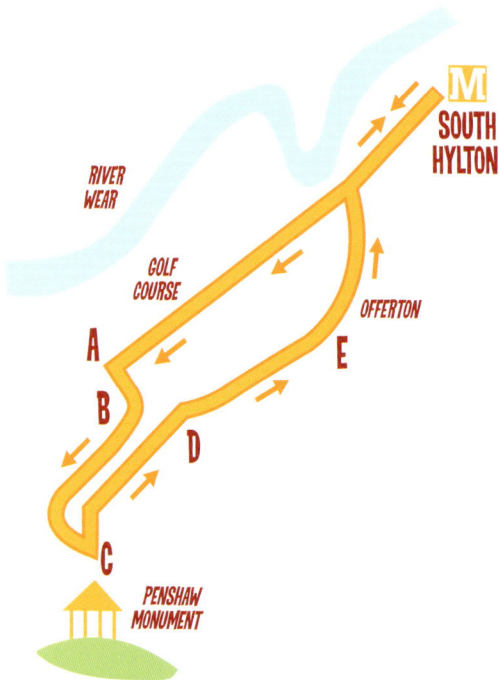

On leaving South Hylton Station continue straight ahead, cross over the road and continue along the path/cycleway which was once a continuation of the railway line. Continue through the underpass beneath the road (A19) and proceed directly ahead, ignoring the path off to the left (you will return down this path). Soon you have woods on your right through which there are glimpses of the River Wear, while on the left there are farm fields. Ahead on your left, from time to time you may be able to see the temple-like structure of Penshaw Monument.

About 800 yards beyond the underpass you come to a junction of paths with The Railway Crossing Cottage on your right. Continue straight ahead for a further 800 yards or so, passing a golf course on your right until you reach a road bridge. **A**

Immediately beyond the bridge, turn right and climb the steps to meet a minor road. Turn right, cross the bridge and walk up the road as it climbs quite steeply. Ahead on the right you will see your destination, Penshaw Monument. As the road bears left you will find a waymarked stile on your right. **B**

(If you wish to avoid the climb to the monument and the stiles, you can continue along the road as from **D** below). Cross the stile and follow the green path as it climbs diagonally towards the woods known as Dawson's Plantation. Go through the gap in the fence into the woods and continue in the same direction along the broad path, ignoring paths off. The path makes its way through the pleasant woods below Penshaw Monument, climbing quite steeply in parts until it exits at a kissing gate onto a track. Turn left and follow the track as it winds round and takes you to some steps leading up to the south side of the monument. Climb up the steps to reach the base of Penshaw Monument. It was erected in 1844 by public subscription in honour of John George Lambton, first Earl of Durham, the first Governor of Canada. This strange anomaly on a Durham hillside was based on the design of an Athenian temple and although rather disappointing on closer inspection, it provides an excellent viewpoint. **C**

After admiring the countryside, take the broad green path on the north side of the monument as it descends with the woods on your left. Bear left to go through a kissing gate at the edge of the woods and continue straight ahead with a wire fence on your right. Cross a waymarked (Wearside Walks) stile and take care as the path narrows over the steep drop. At another waymarked stile the path proceeds ahead along the field edge with the fence now on your left until just beyond the end of the woods where a stile takes you onto the other side of the field boundary. Continue in the same direction as before until you exit onto a minor road at a public footpath sign indicating that you have covered 1/2 mile from Penshaw Monument. **D**

Follow the road up the hill and when the road bears right continue straight ahead in the direction "Offerton only" to pass Offerton Hall Farm on your right. **E**

At the end of the lane, go through the gate and continue along the public bridleway "South Hylton ⅔". Descend the path with the busy road (A19) on your right, glimpses of the River Wear below and the huge Nissan Factory complex beyond on your left. Eventually you arrive at the underpass through which you passed on your outward journey. Go through the underpass and retrace your steps along the disused railway track back to South Hylton Metro Station and the end of the walk.

Penshaw Monument

ROUTE – A pleasant stroll in the countryside down the south side of the River Wear, crossing at Cox Green, continuing on the north side, then returning along the north riverside path and a disused railway line to South Hylton

TERRAIN – Mainly on bridleways and footpaths with some narrow and some steep sections. Parts of the route may be muddy and slippery at times

REFRESHMENTS – Four pubs with varying opening hours

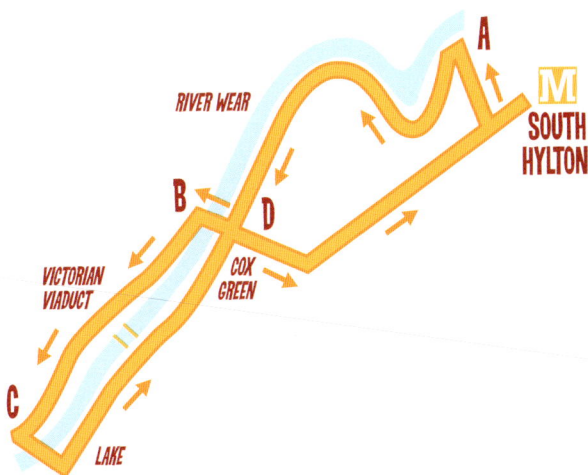

Leave South Hylton Metro Station, cross over the road at the pedestrian lights, with the Hycroft pub on your right and go straight ahead through the metal barrier. Proceed along the broad path that was once a continuation of the railway line, until you reach another metal barrier just before a tunnel under the main road (A19). Turn right and follow the track as it descends between the main road and the houses, ignoring any paths off. At the road junction with the River Wear ahead, turn right and walk some 75 yards to a clearing opposite The Golden Lion. Here you will find a useful information board with details of the history of this area. **A**

Now retrace your steps along the riverside road and proceed straight ahead beneath the road bridge to join a stony track. You pass Riverside Lodge and go over a little footbridge as the track becomes narrower. You now need to follow the riverside path that offers a variety of terrains and surroundings. Birdwatchers should enjoy seeing an interesting selection of birds including herons, cormorants and oystercatchers. When you reach an open area with arable land, the temple-like Penshaw Monument becomes visible on your left, a landmark which will be seen at other points on the walk. You pass a golf course behind a hedgerow on your left and you will also notice a number of "James Steel Park Fitness Trail" signs (James Steel being Chairman of the Washington Development Council 1964- 77) as well as River Wear Trail waymarks.

On the opposite side of the river you will see a landing stage behind which is the large enclosed area of the Washington Wildfowl & Wetlands Centre. The modern building beyond the wildfowl area contains Government offices. A bridge comes into view, you go through a kissing gate and pass a livery yard to go onto a metalled road with stables on your right. Proceed ahead a short distance to the Oddfellows Arms (limited opening times) and the adjacent information board at Cox Green. At the pub there is a road to the left that you will follow later (unless you wish to take a short-cut now and continue the walk from **D** below). To continue on the walk, proceed ahead and cross the River Wear via the footbridge near the old passenger ferry site. **B**

Turn immediately left and walk a short distance to follow the river in the direction of a fingerpost "Victorian Viaduct" and a Cycleway 7 sign. In an open area on the right, a stone bears an inscription relating to the Woodland Trust. When the Cycleway 7 turns right, continue straight ahead by the riverside on the narrow path. Bear left at a junction and go through a metal barrier passing a Woodland Trust sign. As you continue ahead the viaduct comes into view. Pass under the impressive viaduct (1838) and continue ahead to join a metalled lane. After passing a row of houses, the lane meets a main road opposite the welcoming Biddick Inn, behind which is Worm Hill said to be where the legendary Lambton Worm was slain. **C**

To continue on the walk, turn left, cross over the road bridge and turn immediately left down some steps. Continue ahead with the river on your left and some houses on your right. Keep by the riverside to pass the Mount Pleasant Lake and Riverside Area and an information board, You go beneath the Victorian Viaduct again and there are good views of an attractive property on the opposite side of the river. Eventually you return to Cox Green where you turn right at The Oddfellows Arms in the direction "Cox green station". **D**

Climb steadily uphill on the quiet metalled road. Look out for a reminder of local industry behind the metal gates of Church House on your left. Turn left and leave the road at a "Sunderland C2C" sign, about 50 yards before a T-junction. This was an area once occupied by a station and in a short distance you join the track along the dismantled railway. Now continue along the track for about $1\frac{1}{2}$ miles to return to South Hylton Metro Station and the end of the walk.

ROUTE – Along the seafront from Roker, via the marina and the mouth of the River Wear, passing art works, the National Glass Centre and the historic Church of St Peter's at Monkwearmouth

TERRAIN – On the level along metalled paths with one climb via steps or roadway

REFRESHMENTS – Several pubs and coffee shops en route

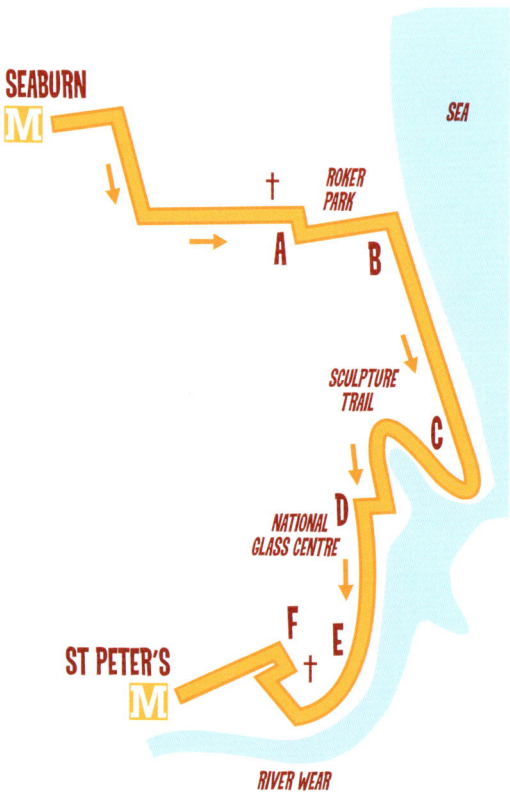

Exit from Seaburn Metro Station, noting on your right Fulwell Windmill a distinctive landmark on the Sunderland horizon for nearly 200 years (open to visitors at certain times). Turn left and follow the B1291 passing the Windmills pub before you reach the traffic lights. Proceed ahead at the lights, then turn

immediately right over Sea Road to go along Fulwell Road
with The Blue Bell on your right. Follow the road for about 400
yards and turn left at Side Cliff Road. Walk along this pleasant
street until you arrive at the crossroads at the corner of Roker
Park (not to be confused with the former Sunderland football
ground). About 100 yards on the left, and well-worth visiting
(Monday-Friday 9am-1pm) is St Andrew's Church, described
as the "cathedral of the Arts and Crafts Movement". **A**

To continue on the walk, turn right, proceed for about 100
yards and cross over the road to enter Roker Park. Follow the
path through the park, passing to the left of the bandstand, to
arrive at an information board at the sea front. **B**

Turn right and walk along the promenade passing The
Smugglers pub. The piers at the mouth of the River Wear lie
ahead and after passing the first pier you soon pass the large
brightly coloured *Banner Belles' Mural/Mosaic* one of the
many public artworks that you will find on this walk. The
promenade leads to the mouth of the Wear, just beyond the
Sunderland Yacht Club, where there is a Royal Bank of
Scotland millennium milepost. **C**

Turn right and follow the riverside path with excellent views of
the river on your left and ahead. It is difficult to imagine that
this river was not very long ago the location of a thriving
shipbuilding industry. The path winds its way around a marina
where you will see some metal birds and some interesting
stone carvings, part of the St Peter's Riverside Sculpture
Project. You pass the Marine Activities Centre where a plaque
commemorates fallen members of the Royal and Merchant
Navy. The Snow Goose Gift and Coffee Shop lies to the right.
Just beyond the RNLI office you find further examples of public
artworks. Continue by the riverside until the path comes to a
dead-end at a car parking area. Climb the 58 steps away
from the river and bear left to meet another path. (To avoid the
steps follow the access road (Beacon Drive), turn left at the
T-junction, go up the road and turn left just before the BP filling
station to meet the path reached from the steps). **D**

Now follow the path as it gradually descends back towards
the river. You pass a bench on your right with a railed viewing
area on the left opposite the Fina oil depot. About 30 yards
further on, turn right then left to detour via the sculpture *The
Red House*. Go through the "house" to rejoin the riverside
path, turn right and walk ahead. Take the left-hand fork to

descend to meet the river and arrive at the National Glass Centre. You might then like to visit the Glass Centre where refreshments are also available. **E**

Continue along the riverside path that soon passes some University of Sunderland buildings. The aptly named sculpture *Pathways of Knowledge* stands in front of The Prospect Building opened in 1993 by the President of the European Parliament. Proceed ahead for about 100 yards towards the large metal sculpture *Shadows in Another Light* with Wearmouth Bridge and the adjacent rail bridge just beyond. Before reaching the sculpture, turn right onto the metalled path that climbs away from the riverside. St Peter's Church appears ahead on the right. Proceed to a T-junction at Wearbank House, turn right and walk to a further T-junction. Cross the road and turn left to the entrance to the church grounds. An information board just beyond the gates gives a few details about the historic church of St Peter's, first built in AD674 (open for visitors Easter to October on weekdays 2.00-4.30pm). **F**

Leave the church grounds, turn right and walk a few yards to a T-junction with a busy road (Dame Dorothy Street). Turn left and walk for about 500 yards to the traffic lights. Proceed ahead via two sets of pedestrian lights to St Peter's Metro Station and the end of the walk.

ROUTE – Across Wearmouth Bridge and around Sunderland centre including Mowbray Gardens and Sunderland Minster

TERRAIN – On the level along pavements and metalled paths. There is one flight of steps which can be avoided

REFRESHMENTS – A wide choice of refreshment places throughout the walk including cafes at Sunderland Museum and Sunderland Minster

Leave St. Peter's Metro Station and turn left. Walk the short distance to the Monkwearmouth Station Museum. The colonnaded portico was the impressive entrance to the original main line station. If time permits, a visit to this fascinating museum is well worthwhile. Admission is free. There's lots to see for children and grown ups and it's a must for railway buffs. From the museum, retrace your steps towards the Metro Station, then proceed ahead towards Wearmouth Bridge. Just before the bridge there is a plaque which gives details of its history. Cross the bridge. Another plaque explains the significance of this location in the Civil War (1644). After a few yards turn left and cross the road by a series of traffic lights to the church opposite. Turn left, then right, and walk ahead with the church on your right. St Mary's R.C. Church is an early example (1830-35) of the building of a Catholic church, following the Catholic Emancipation Act of 1829. Proceed along the road (Bridge Street) to the crossroads. Cross the road to the building opposite, the intriguing Elephant Tea Rooms (1873) built for a tea merchant and described by its architect, Frank Caws, as in the "Hindoo Gothic" style. Turn left to cross Fawcett Street and proceed ahead along High Street West to its junction with West Sunniside. **A**

Turn right and walk along West Sunniside. In recent years the street has been carefully renovated by the Council in an attempt to recapture its Victorian ambience. The former General Post Office (1903) is on the left. On the right, at the junction with St Thomas Street there are two buildings in the art nouveau style. At the end of the road turn right, then left and go along Foyle Street. At the T-junction, turn right. Walk to the crossroads and turn left into Toward Road. Walk a few yards to the entrance to Mowbray Gardens on your right. **B**

Go into the park. The tall column of the Sunderland War Memorial is ahead and the Sunderland Museum and Winter Gardens is on the right. Admission is free. It is well worth visiting the museum and experiencing the rebuilt winter gardens (opened in 2001). In Mowbray Gardens there are a number of memorials. From the museum, these include, over to the left, a memorial to 183 children who died in a tragic accident in 1883 and, higher up over to the right, a statue of Jack Crawford (1795-1857) whose story makes interesting reading. Walk through the park to the highest point, Building Hill, on a rocky outcrop. At the summit there is a statue of General H. Havelock, a national hero who was born in Bishopwearmouth. From here there are splendid views of the sea and the mouth of the River Wear. You need to descend towards the church, which is just beyond the park. To avoid steps you will need to bear left and at the bottom of the slope turn right and walk parallel to the road with the park railings on your left. Exit from the park gate. **C**

Cross the road to Park Road Methodist Church (1887). Turn

right and cross to the other side of the road. Now turn left to walk along Douro Terrace with houses from the 1850s. On the left, the tall St Bede Tower, now part of the University of Sunderland, was originally built for the mayor in 1852. You arrive at a telephone box on your right. Ahead, the former Christ Church (1864) is now occupied by the Sikh Association. Ahead, on the left is Langham Tower (1889) also part of the University of Sunderland. Turn right at the telephone box and walk to Esplanade West. Turn right. On your right are the splendid properties of The Esplanade (1853-60) overlooking their private garden. Walk along Esplanade West. At a convenient point, cross the road and proceed ahead. On the left is a red sandstone church with an unusual and imposing tower. Originally St George's Presbyterian Church (1890), it is now St George's with Trinity and St James United Reformed Church. Carry on along Grange Terrace. You arrive at a busy road intersection. Opposite is an entrance to Park Lane Metro Station. **D**

Turn right to cross the road at the pedestrian crossing. Turn left and walk ahead for about 60 yards and turn left into Mary Street. Walk to the end of the street and bear right to cross at the pedestrian lights into Albion Place. Walk a short distance then turn left to cross the road at a further set of pedestrian lights. Then turn right and cross to the other side of Green Terrace. There are direction signs on the corner for the Empire Theatre and the Minster. Turn left. On the right is the ornate red brick Galen Building, the original Technical College (1900) which developed into the University of Sunderland. On the left is the University's Priestman Building (1939), financed by Sir John Priestman, a local shipbuilder and benefactor. Continue ahead and cross a road at traffic lights then immediately turn right. Walk a few yards and turn left into the open area. Walk ahead. The Mowbray Almshouses (1863), built on the site of the Gibson Almshouses of 1727, are on the right. Go through the gateway on your left into the grounds of Sunderland Minster. **E**

The visitors' entrance is a few yards ahead on the right. Inside the church, the Clock Tower Coffee Shop is a pleasant refreshment stop. The Minster Church of St Michael and All Angels, formerly Bishopwearmouth Parish Church, was inaugurated as Sunderland Minster in 1998 following Sunderland's elevation to city status in 1992. The church has a long history. The present building has a 19th century tower and other features but is mainly the result of a sensitive reconstruction in 1933-35, with funds provided by Sir John Priestman. Leave the church and turn left to walk towards the almshouses. Turn left and walk along the lane (Church Lane) to a road on the other side of which is The Empire Theatre (1906). Turn right and walk ahead towards the triangular-shaped Londonderry pub. Cross the road to walk along the pavement with the pub on your left. At the T-junction turn left and walk ahead. Cross the road and at the corner turn right onto the pedestrian/cyclist path to the right of the little green ahead. Follow the path the short distance and cross a busy road to enter a pedestrianised street. You need to be careful here because the street is intersected by vehicular roads. Continue to the end of the pedestrianised section and walk to the Elephant Tea Rooms on your right. Turn right into Fawcett Street and walk ahead. Turn right at the Northern Rock building and walk ahead to Sunderland Metro Station and the end of the walk. The Metro trains run from platforms 2 and 3.

Mowbray Park & Winter Gardens

Leave Sunderland Metro Station, passing Milligans Patisserie on your right, and turn left. Walk a short distance to Fawcett Street and turn left. Continue ahead, passing, on your left, the City of Sunderland Tourist Information Centre where the friendly staff are always happy to advise. Despite its obvious lack of uniformity, the street contains several interesting buildings. At the crossroads (with your last café-bistro ahead) use the traffic lights to turn right into High Street West. Proceed for a short distance and turn left at the next set of lights to walk ahead passing Cineworld on your right. Just before the T-junction, bear left to follow the subway sign. At the bottom of the ramp turn right to go through the subway with the mural of local scenes on either side. At the exit, bear right towards the bridge to pass, on your right, a blue plaque giving some details of Pann's Bank. Proceed across Wearmouth Bridge taking time to admire the view of the University buildings over to your right, beyond which is the National Glass Centre. At the far end of the bridge, a further blue plaque gives some information about the bridge's antecedents. If you don't mind a lot of steps then take the steps to the immediate right of the blue plaque to descend to the riverside path. **A** (Otherwise continue ahead, passing St Peter's Metro Station on your left and bear right to leave the main road and descend past St Peter's Wharf apartments. Follow the cycleway signs to arrive at the riverside path).

Turn right and walk ahead to pass beneath Wearmouth Bridge. After a covered archway, bear left to continue ahead with the river close-by on your left. You pass a crossing of paths and after a further 200 yards or so, as the River Wear bears to the right, you will find a number of castings set into the path. These serve as a reminder that you are now walking over an area once famed for its deep coal mines. Look for the references to the fossils found below as well as the interesting tale of the mother who only slept in her bed at weekends! Above, to the right, you can catch glimpses of the Stadium of Light, home of Sunderland FC since 1997. You soon come to the remains of some kilns on your right which date from around 1800 and which used stone from the nearby quarries at Carley Hill. A number of plaques on the walls relate to the industrial heritage of the area. After a further couple of hundred yards you arrive at a sign for C2C Cycleway 7 and a path to the right. **B**

Bear right to follow the path as it climbs away from the riverside. Pass through a metal barrier and bear left to follow the cycleway sign through another barrier. Walk ahead and after about hundred yards turn right to follow the C2C sign and climb steeply for a short distance before turning left at a T-junction. Now follow the track ahead. You pass beneath a road bridge, some 50 yards beyond which, you need to leave the main path and turn left. Walk a short distance to the main road. Continue in the same direction to cross the road via the pedestrian lights and turn immediately right to use further lights to cross over the approach road to the Queen Alexandra Bridge. Turn left, walk across the bridge and follow the pavement as it bears right at the T junction. **C**

Now continue in the same direction passing the Gala Bingo on your left and crossing a road bridge over the Metro line before you eventually reach Pallion Metro Station and the end of the walk.

Stadium of Light

Pallion to South Hylton
(3 miles)

↗ **ROUTE** – Follows the direction of the Metro line through pleasant countryside with the River Wear generally close at hand.

🚶 **TERRAIN** – On footpaths and tracks some of which can be muddy at times

☕ **REFRESHMENTS** – Three pubs near the end of the walk

Exit from Pallion Metro Station Platform 1 and turn right. From Platform 2 take the bridge over the Metro line and turn right. Walk along the pavement with a shopping complex below on the right. This area was once the site of the Pallion Shipyards and renowned Doxfords marine engineering works. After several hundred yards as the road bears left at a roundabout, bear right and follow a public footpath sign to go under the bridge carrying the Metro line. **A**

Continue along the track, which can be muddy at times, with metal railings on your right and the Metro line on your left. At the end of the metal railings on your right, turn right and follow the line of the railings down the grassy bank towards the river. In the distance on the opposite side of the river you may catch a glimpse of Hylton Castle amid the trees. At the bottom of the bank, about 40 yards before the end of the railings, bear left to find a narrow path between the bushes. Sometimes tyre marks indicate the way! **B**

Follow the narrow path, often muddy and slippery, as it descends towards the riverside. The path levels off as it becomes a wider track and over to the left are some limestone cliffs. When the track reaches a metalled roadway, turn right and follow the metalled path past Hylton Sea Scouts hut and a small marina. **C**

After passing a number of benches from where you can sit and admire the bird life of the river area, the path narrows and climbs quite steeply for a short distance. At a fork bear left to keep on the main path. Soon, on your right, you pass an information board (sadly defaced at the time of writing). Ignore a road off to the left and continue to follow the riverside path. There are some interesting sights on the opposite side of the river: pleasant properties, remains of old boats and the Shipwrights pub. This was the site of a ferry crossing from the 12th century until 1957. Now its modern-day replacement, the Hylton Bridge (1974) is clearly in view. Continue along the riverside towards the bridge, ignoring paths off to arrive at an information board in front of The Golden Lion pub. D

Walk towards the pub and turn right. After about 75 yards, just before the bridge, turn left and climb away from the river on the steep track. Ignore paths off until you come to a T-junction. Turn left and follow the track a few hundred yards to the main road. On your left is The Hycroft pub and a little further down the road on the right is The Jolly Potter. Cross the road with care to South Hylton Metro Station and the end of the walk.

ROUTE - From Seaburn to Whitburn and on to the water tower on Cleadon Hills. Then via Cleadon to East Boldon

TERRAIN - On a variety of metalled paths and field tracks. Mainly on the level with one long gradual ascent

REFRESHMENTS - Pubs in Seaburn, tea room and pubs in Whitburn and a pub near East Boldon Metro station

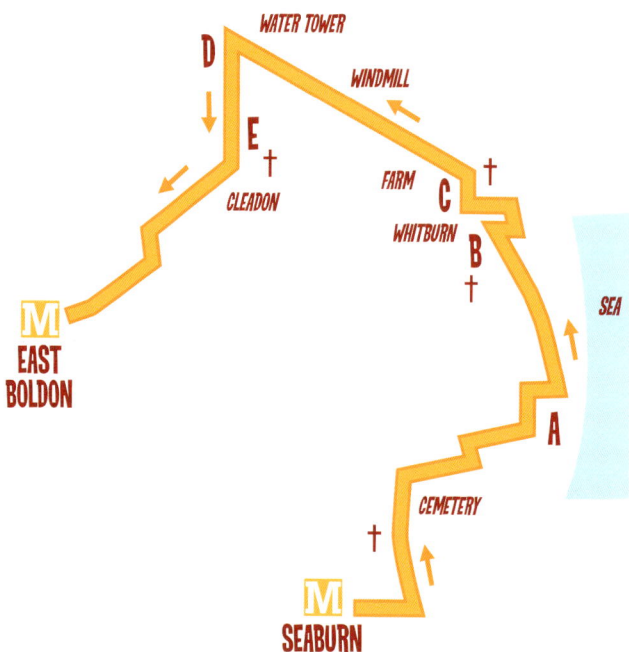

WATER TOWER

D

WINDMILL

E †

CLEADON

FARM

C †

WHITBURN

B †

SEA

M
EAST
BOLDON

A

CEMETERY

†

M
SEABURN

Leave Seaburn Metro Station, turn left and walk ahead, passing the Fire Station on your right. At the traffic lights go straight over and turn left. Proceed ahead to a roundabout. Carry on past the roundabout and, just before Fulwell Methodist Church, take the service road on the right and go through the South West Lodge gate into the cemetery (Mere Knolls). Turn left and walk along the path with the boundary wall on your left. Turn right at West Lodge and keep on the broad path as it gently ascends. On the left you pass a memorial to the Sunderland civilians who lost their lives through enemy action in the Second World War. Continue past the cemetery chapels, now gently descending. At the bottom, where the broad path turns right, bear left and walk the short distance to a footbridge. Cross the bridge and turn right. Proceed ahead via a metal barrier and carry on to meet a road. Continue for a few yards then cross the road and go through the blue railings onto a metalled pathway. Walk ahead, passing an interesting children's play area on your right. Bear slightly left to avoid the car park and carry straight on. At the end of the path, turn right. Follow the path as it bears left and runs along the edge of the grassland on the left. The path emerges onto a road in a housing estate. Turn right and proceed along Cleveland View. Where the road bears left, go straight ahead on the footpath to arrive at the sea front. **A**

Turn left and walk ahead. Just before the South Tyneside sign turn left and go along the public footpath to Whitburn. Exit from the path onto a narrow road and continue in the same direction. On your left you pass Red Cottage (1843), by John and Benjamin Green, celebrated 19th-century architects whose work includes the Theatre Royal, Newcastle, and Penshaw Monument. A few yards further on is Whitburn Parish Church (a medieval church restored in the 1860s). The road joins a busy road with attractive greens on both sides. **B**

Turn right and walk along the main road (Front Street) to come to The Village Café, which has a tea room. At the junction turn left and go along East Street and then left again along North Guards. Pass Whitburn Methodist Church on your right and in a short distance turn right and walk along Wellands Lane. After about half a mile, turn left onto the public footpath. (A notice makes it clear that this path is for walkers, not cyclists). **C**

The path is mainly well-defined and waymarked. Walk ahead, soon passing between farm buildings. Carry on to the corner of a hedgerow and turn right to go over a stile, with a waymark indicating that you are on a South Tyneside circular walk. Carry on and cross another stile. Follow the path as it gradually ascends and eventually bears left and you go over another stile. Further on the lower section of Cleadon Windmill and the tall Cleadon Water Tower (1862) come into view; they are prominent landmarks for miles around. The tower was built, as part of the former pumping station, in the Italianate style by Sir Thomas Hawksley, the noted water engineer. Keep aiming for the windmill. There are splendid panoramic views to enjoy from here. Looking south, Penshaw Monument is a notable feature. When you reach the windmill you can read an outline of its history on the plaques displayed inside. Now walk towards the tower, with a stone wall on your right. Go through the kissing gate and turn immediately left. Walk down to a lane and continue the short distance to a junction. **D**

Turn left and walk down the road (Sunniside Lane) past fields and then housing. The first property on the right, now Oakleigh Gardens School, was Cleadon Cottage Homes (1909-1968), providing vocational training for orphan boys and girls. Keep walking left at junctions. You come to a T-junction. **E**

All Saints Church (1869) with its white bellcote is on the left. Cross the road and bear right, past the Cleadon Pond, where an information board gives some interesting details. Cross Sunderland Road and continue along Front Street with the Beefeater pub on your right and the Cleadon War Memorial on your left. After the shops you pass the red brick Cleadon House (1738) on your left. A little further on, on the right, you see Cleadon Primary School and then a bus stop. A few yards further on, turn left at the corner of a hedge and walk towards the house. You come to a public footpath sign tucked away to the left of the house. Go onto the public footpath. Follow the path which runs between garden fences. At a junction, bear right. Continue until you join East Boldon Road at a junction with a main road. Walk ahead along the main road for a few hundred yards to East Boldon Metro Station and the end of the walk.

WALK 18

East Boldon to Carley Hill to Seaburn (3 miles)

ROUTE – On a road and footpaths through Cleadon, then across country via Carley Hill and Fulwell Windmill to Seaburn

TERRAIN – Mostly on the level on pavements, field paths and surfaced tracks with several gentle climbs. There is a descent down a fairly steep short flight of steps near the end of the walk

REFRESHMENTS – A pub near East Boldon Metro Station and one near the end of the walk

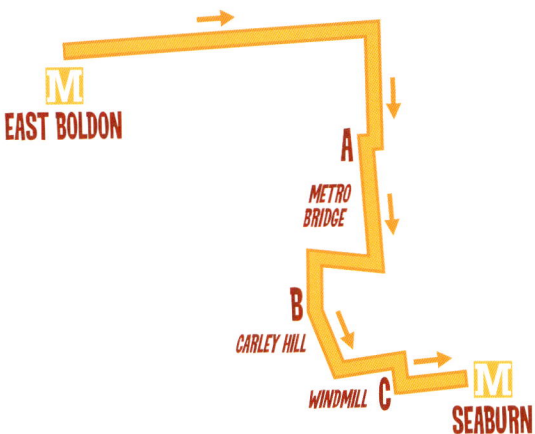

M EAST BOLDON

A

METRO BRIDGE

B

CARLEY HILL

WINDMILL C

M SEABURN

Exit East Boldon Metro Station and turn right. Walk ahead, passing Sleepers pub and restaurant. Continue on the main road (B1299) for about ³/₄ mile, between a wide variety of interesting properties. About 150 yards after passing Laburnum Grove on your left, look for a public footpath sign on your right. Go onto the path and walk ahead to exit onto a road. Continue in the same direction along Woodlands Drive and then carry on along the public footpath ahead to meet a road. Cross the road to come to a public footpath sign a few yards on your right. A

Go onto the path. Soon you are walking along a field boundary with a hedgerow on your right. Eventually, the path goes under a Metro bridge and exits at a busy road. Turn right and walk on the pavement for about ¹/₄ mile. Just beyond the South Tyneside sign, with extreme care cross the busy road to join the bridleway just to the right of Lowland Cottage.

Walk ahead. The path narrows and gently ascends to a T-junction with another path. Turn left and walk a few yards to a junction of paths with a collection of signs. **B**

Turn right, through a metal gateway, in the direction "Carley Hill" and proceed on the path, as it climbs between wooded areas then levels out through more open country. Eventually you walk alongside metal railings with the houses of Carley Hill over to your right. Follow the path as it bears left. Keep to the main path which passes through a metal barrier and runs between metal railings. Cleadon Water Tower can be seen in the distance on your left and the sails of Fulwell Windmill appear on the right and you pass evidence of former quarrying. You come to a large boulder to the right of which is the housing of a World War 1 coastal watch mirror, with an explanatory plaque. Soon you reach a large white gate on the right where there is a "Beware of the dog" sign. Turn right and walk up the grassy area to the left of the white gate. Continue on the path through a short section of woodland before emerging into an open area. There are good views of the sea from here. The remains of Fulwell Quarry limekilns are on the left. Walk ahead towards the building below the windmill and descend via a flight of fairly steep steps to join the pavement near the entrance to Fulwell Windmill (1808). **C**

The mill is open to the public on Saturdays and Sundays from 12 – 4. If time permits you may wish to visit the mill and, if wind conditions are right, you may see the milling process in action. To continue the walk, proceed ahead, with the mill on your right, to the busy crossroads. The Grange pub is ahead. You need to turn left and cross the road at the traffic lights. Continue ahead to Seaburn Metro Station and the end of the walk.

Fulwell Windmill

ROUTE – Along pleasant footpaths to Boldon Colliery, then via the Colliery Wood recreation area to Brockley Whins

TERRAIN – Mainly on the level along metalled paths

REFRESHMENTS – A pub in Boldon Colliery and a cafe at Asda

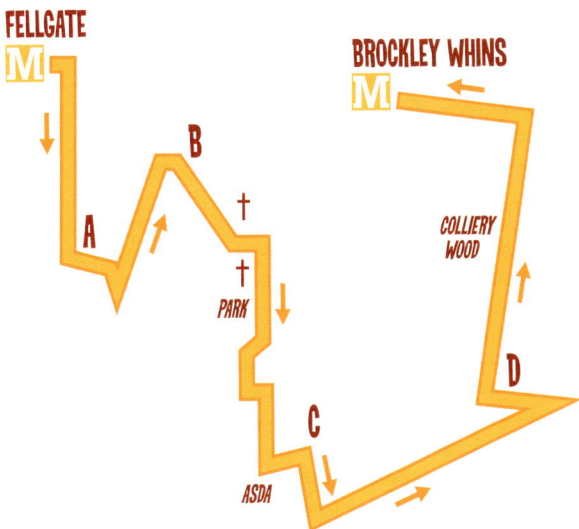

FELLGATE

BROCKLEY WHINS

A

B

†

†

PARK

COLLIERY WOOD

D

C

ASDA

Leave Fellgate Metro Station. From Platform 1, take the stairs or lift and bear left to join the road and walk under the Metro bridge. Turn left to pick up the metalled path. From Platform 2, take the stairs or lift to join the metalled path and turn left. Proceed ahead on the path, parallel to the Metro line, and at the fork bear right. Keep on the path as it descends to the narrow Calfclose Burn and, ignoring paths off, follow the burn. When the path meets a road at a T-junction turn right and walk a few yards to a bus stop. Turn left, cross the road and continue ahead on the metalled path now with the burn on your left. You arrive at a footbridge. **A**

Cross the footbridge and then bear right to cross Fieldway and continue in the same direction, passing Brookfield Park on your right. Follow the road as it curves, until shortly after a sports court you reach Moorlands on your right. Turn right, cross over the road and walk to the end of Moorlands. Turn left and walk along the path with houses on your left. When you reach the last bungalow, don't follow the path to the left. Instead, bear right, then walk a few yards and turn right to cross the bridge over the main road (A19). Bear right, walk a few yards, then turn left to cross the road at the traffic island to arrive at a junction with Hedworth Lane. **B**

Proceed along Hedworth Lane, passing Aged Miners Homes on both sides. Follow the road as it bears left and passes St Nicholas' Church, Hedworth (1878) on your left. Continue in the same direction; Hedworth Lane Methodist Church (1895) appears on your right. A short distance before The Crown pub, cross the road with care and go along the road to the left of the church. Turn right and then almost immediately left to enter the little park (Coronation Park). Walk ahead and exit through the gate on your right. Walk straight ahead across the road and on the pavement between the houses. When you reach a path ahead, turn left and walk towards Simpson Close. Carry on in the same direction on the metalled path. Turn left then immediately right through wooden barriers into the recreation ground. At the T-junction, turn left and proceed ahead. Take the second path on the right, walk to a circle and bear left. Walk ahead, ignoring paths off, and exit the recreation ground. Turn right and come to a roundabout near Asda. Turn left to cross the road with care and go into a small clearing with benches. Walk past an unusual wrought iron war memorial and join the main road. Cross the road at the traffic lights. Turn right and walk to North Road. **C**

To continue the walk, proceed along the left-hand side of North Road. You pass a parade of shops, including the RU Peckish sandwich bar and deli, and houses. On your right is the Boldon British Legion Club with its memorial clock and plaque. After passing Watson Terrace, as the road enters open country, continue ahead for about 150 yards. Turn left through the metal barrier and then almost immediately left again to join a metalled path. Follow the path, with the narrow River Don on your left, ignoring paths off, until you reach a fork at a metal bench with housing ahead. Bear left and proceed ahead for several hundred yards, again ignoring paths off, until you reach a crossing of paths beside a metal bench behind houses. Turn left and follow the path as it crosses a footbridge. Bear right and walk for 100 yards to reach a main road (New

Road). Turn left and walk for 300 yards to the entrance to Boldon Comprehensive School. Turn right and cross the road with care to take the public footpath opposite. **D**

Follow the surfaced track as it makes its way round the playing fields on your left. To the right, in the distance, you can see the tall Cleadon Water Tower (1862) and the base of Cleadon Windmill. Where the track forks, bear left at a public bridleway sign to pass a small pond on your right. You are now in Colliery Wood, land reclaimed after the closure of Boldon Colliery. The small metal sculpture near the pond is one of twelve forming a children's sculpture trail. Walk along the broad track until you reach a T-junction beside some metal sculptures. Turn right and walk ahead. At a crossing of paths continue straight ahead. Go through a metal barrier and, after a few yards, bear right and follow the path as it descends to arrive near a former railway bridge on your right. Cross a footbridge and bear right for a few yards, then turn left and follow the main path to arrive at Brockley Whins Metro Station and the end of the walk.

Brockley Whins to East Boldon
(3.5 miles)

ROUTE – A meander through the Boldons: Boldon Colliery, New Town, West Boldon, East Boldon, passing a wide variety of residential properties

TERRAIN – On metalled paths and pavements. At the beginning there is a steep descent and a climb, thereafter mostly on the level with one long, gradual ascent

REFRESHMENTS – A pub in Boldon Colliery, a cafe at Asda, two pubs in West Boldon and a pub near East Boldon Metro Station

Exit Brockley Whins Metro Station: from Platform 1, turn right to cross the bridge over the Metro line and go straight ahead down the steep metalled path; from Platform 2, turn left, walk to the bridge then turn right and walk straight ahead down the metalled path. Cross the footbridge and carry straight on. The path runs along the boundary of Colliery Wood, a recreational area reclaimed from the former Boldon Colliery, and you may see some small metal sculptures, part of a children's sculpture trail. At a crossing of paths, (where the path ahead goes up broad steps), take the path on the right. Follow this to exit at a road. Cross the road and carry on in the same direction. The path meets a road at The Colliery Tavern in Boldon Colliery. **A**

Turn left and proceed ahead. Here you have the traditional street of a Durham mining community, with terraces of cottages with long front gardens. The houses in The Terrace were occupied by mine officials. Cross to the other side of the road at a convenient point. Further on you pass other examples of mining village institutions: the Bolton Ale House, an Independent Methodist church (1885) and an old-fashioned police station. At the end of the road, bear right to walk a short distance to a roundabout. Asda is ahead. Turn left, cross the road with care, and walk ahead, past the little park area on the left, to traffic lights. Cross the road, turn right then left into North Road. Walk ahead, past houses and a parade of shops, and turn left into Wilfred Street. This area, a development beyond Boldon Colliery, is known as New Town. **B**

Proceed along Wilfred Street and, just after South Crescent on the left, bear right and take the path to the right of the "No horse riding" sign. Ahead you may catch a glimpse of the steeple of the church at West Boldon, a notable landmark and your next destination. Cross the footbridge and go up the path between the houses. Go straight ahead up Hillside, turn right at the T-junction to walk along Boldon Drive. Turn left and walk up Prospect Gardens. Go up some steps then turn right and walk along the short alleyway between houses. Turn left and follow the path to a road. Take time to look back to appreciate the fine views of South Tyneside. Cross the road and continue on the path ahead to emerge near the 13th-century church of St Nicholas in West Boldon. The church is built on the top of a small hill and is visible for miles around. **C**

Turn right and walk ahead with the church wall on your left. Carry on along Rectory Bank, then bear left, past the Black Horse and The Wheatsheaf pubs on the right, to arrive at a main road (A184). Use the pedestrian lights to cross over the road. Turn left and walk a few yards then turn right into Hylton Lane and proceed ahead. Turn into the first street on the left, Dipe Lane, and walk ahead. You pass Boldon Cemetery on your right. When it is convenient cross to the pavement on the other side. Go past the entrance to Boldon Golf Club. Here, and a little further on, on the other side of the road, signs indicate that you are leaving West Boldon and entering East Boldon. **D**

Follow the road, passing some interesting properties. After the road takes a sharp turn to the left it becomes Bridle Path. Carry on and take the next road on the right, South Lane.

After about 500 yards or so, just after a sign for a school, follow the road as it turns left at a one way sign to arrive at a main road (A184). Turn right and walk ahead, passing St George the Martyr Church (1923) on your right. Proceed past the War Memorial. Cross Whitburn Terrace and continue to the traffic lights. Turn left to cross the road and bear right into Station Road. Proceed ahead to East Boldon Metro Station and the end of the walk.

➤ **ROUTE** – Along both sides of the Tyne, west of Gateshead and Newcastle mainly close to the river and including some surprisingly green areas amid the industrial sections

🚶 **TERRAIN** – On metalled paths with a short section on a stony track and with two steep climbs

☕ **REFRESHMENTS** – Two pubs en route and a cafe/bar in Newcastle Business Park as well as plenty of choice near both Metro stations

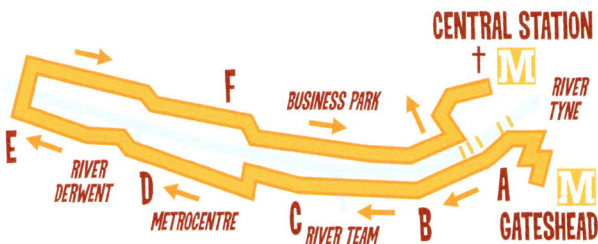

Leave Gateshead Metro Station by the West Street North exit and follow the ramp to the main road (West Street). Turn left and proceed downhill passing a large sculpture *Sports Day* by Mike Winstone (1986). Cross over to the other side of the road at the earliest opportunity to pass the old post office, the site of a house where the famous engraver and naturalist Thomas Bewick (1753-1828) lived and died. A short distance further on you pass an ornate clock of 1892 in front of the old Town Hall (1868). Continue downhill, cross the road via the pedestrian lights, go under the railway bridge, turn right, walk under another bridge to reach a road leading to the Tyne Bridge. Turn left, cross the road and descend in the direction of the slip road to pass the Hilton Hotel before arriving at the approach to a low-level bridge, the Swing Bridge (1868-76). Don't cross the bridge but instead turn left along Pipewellgate and continue ahead passing beneath the High Level Bridge built by Robert Stephenson and Thomas Harrison in 1845-49. Turn right just beyond the blue railings of the premises of Gateshead sea cadets to join the riverside path. **A**

Now proceed ahead with splendid views across the Tyne on your right. You may also see some metal sculptures on your left before passing beneath the Queen Elizabeth II Metro Bridge (1976-1980). You pass beneath the King Edward VII Rail

Bridge (1902-6) and then the Redheugh Bridge (1980-83). Continue along the riverside path until eventually you reach a housing complex (Staiths South Bank). The path leads to an open area and on the right are remnants of the wooden staithes originally used for loading boats with coal. Turn left and follow the road (Autumn Drive) between the houses to the junction with the main road. **B**

Turn right and continue in the direction of the main road. For the next couple of miles look out for the signs for the Keelman's Way and Cycleway 14 as you walk through a built-up area but one that is not without its distractions. A large amount of new housing is being built along the south bank of the Tyne and there is no access to the river for some considerable distance. You find, for a short while, that you are accompanied by the River Team before it bears right to flow into the Tyne. You pass the Riverside Lodge on your left. Carry on along the pavement passing the Tudor Rose on your right. Shortly after the new Riverside Park housing development, turn right at Dunston Workshops and walk for about 60 yards to the entrance to Jewson's building materials yard. **C**

Take a narrow path on the left immediately before the gates and continue ahead on the cycleway for a few hundred yards to rejoin the pavement at Handy Drive. Soon the River Tyne comes back into view with the Newcastle Business Park, which you will pass on your return journey, on the opposite bank. Turn right and then left along the cycleway as it leaves the roadside again. Continue ahead for a few hundred yards until the path returns to the road at a junction where there is a railway bridge on the other side of the road. Cross the busy road with care and go under the bridge. Turn immediately right and follow the narrow path. The Keelman's Way passes under two further bridges, with the vast MetroCentre shopping and entertainment complex clearly visible on the left. The path continues through a pleasant tree-lined and green area until it eventually comes adjacent to the Newcastle to Carlisle railway and passes beneath a road bridge. Proceed ahead until you reach a metal footbridge over the River Derwent. **D**

Cross over the bridge, then turn immediately left to descend a short flight of steps (alternatively use the ramp a short distance ahead) and turn sharp left to pass under the bridge and arrive at the riverside. Scotswood Bridge, which you will use to cross over the Tyne, is clearly visible ahead. Continue along the bank of the Tyne, walk over the slipway and detour a short way past the marina service outlets on your right before returning to the riverside. Continue for a few hundred yards and then bear left for "Newcastle via Scotswood Bridge". Proceed up the ramp and walk across the bridge. An information board gives some details about its history. **E**

Follow the pavement as it bears right to arrive at a footbridge. Go up the ramp and cross to the other side of the road. At the end of the bridge at a junction of paths turn right to follow Cycleway 72 which will take you back to the quayside in Newcastle. The metalled path goes through a pleasant green area, once the site of terraces of houses leading down to Newcastle's famous Scotswood Road. Eventually the cycleway joins the pavement alongside the road. Continue in the same direction taking care while crossing Whitehouse Road. Walk ahead for a few hundred yards until you reach some traffic lights. Turn right and cross over the road to enter William Armstrong Drive with the Newcastle Business Park on your left. Follow the road for about 400 yards as it descends towards the river to arrive at a Royal Bank of Scotland milepost. Here there is also the first of a series of information boards about Lord Armstrong, his engineering works and the industrial heritage of the Scotswood-Elswick area. **F**

Take the right-hand fork to join the riverside walkway. Continue from here and enjoy the views. Ahead on the horizon, to the right of a tall block of flats, you may even be able to see the outstretched wings of Antony Gormley's famous sculpture *Angel of the North*. You pass several information boards, sculptures and seats and you have the possibility of refreshments at the Bar Escape. Eventually the bridges come back into view and when you reach the Metro Bridge, a short distance before the Copthorne Hotel, you need to leave the riverside and turn left in the direction "Central Station". Cross the road with care and climb the steep Forth Banks. Bear left at the top to go under a bridge where half-way under you will find a pedestrian crossing. Cross the road with great care, turn left and then turn right to walk up Central Parkway. On your left is the Centre for Life with its genetics, science and education resources. At the road junction turn right and walk ahead. On your left you will see St Mary's RC Cathedral (Pugin 1842-4) and then the bronze sculpture by Nigel Boonham, unveiled by the Queen during her Jubilee Tour in May 2002, of Cardinal Basil Hume, a noted spiritual leader and a popular Novocastrian. Continue beneath the Central Station portico to arrive at the Metro Station and the end of the walk.

Gateshead to Saltwell Park to Gateshead (3.5 miles)

ROUTE – A circular, urban walk with several cultural points of interest, including Shipley Art Gallery, and a visit to Saltwell Park where the walk may be extended

TERRAIN – Largely on the level, along pavements, with one long gradual climb

REFRESHMENTS – Two hotels, several pubs en route and a café in Saltwell Park

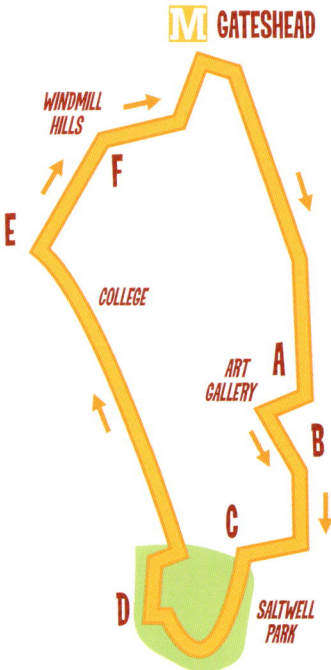

Ⓜ GATESHEAD

WINDMILL HILLS

F

E

COLLEGE

ART GALLERY

A

B

C

D

SALTWELL PARK

Leave Gateshead Metro Station by the West Street North exit and walk up the ramp to the main road (West Street). Turn right and continue straight ahead on the pavement. You very soon reach a church (St Joseph's RC) where you should look for a sculpture beside the bushes at the corner of Walker Terrace. Then you pass the Registrar's Offices on your right and a police station and Royal Mail offices on your left, before reaching the Swallow Hotel on your right. A few hundred yards after the hotel, just before a bus shelter and some traffic lights, leave the pavement to enter a small park area on your right. **A**

Take the right-hand fork and follow the path to the road ahead. Turn left and walk a few yards to a pedestrian crossing. Cross the road to the Central Library, turn left and walk a few yards to some traffic lights. (On the other hand, you may wish to visit the Tourist Information Office and attractive Gallery housed in the Library, the entrance to which is on the right). To continue on the walk, cross over the road and proceed a short distance in the same direction to the Shipley Art Gallery. Admission to the gallery is free and it contains some fine paintings and items of local history. Even if time is pressing you might at least like to see W.C. Irving's painting *Blaydon Races - A study from life*. Outside, to the left of the gallery, stands a splendid statue of a local sporting hero, James Renforth, with information about his exploits and tragic death recorded on the plinth. **B**

To continue on the walk proceed ahead from the gallery to meet a junction with the main road (Durham Road). On your left, stands a substantial memorial, within which "are recorded the names of the men of Gateshead who gave their lives in the Great War 1914-19". Turn right, continue ahead and after passing the Springfield Hotel on your left and a small parade of shops on your right, turn right and descend Enfield Road as far as the Little Theatre. Cross over the road and go into Saltwell Park. **C**

This Victorian park is the site of Saltwell Towers once the home of William Wailes (1808 -1888) the noted manufacturer of stained glass. The park has been the subject of a major restoration of its landscape, buildings and monuments to bring it back to its former glory as "The People's Park". There is plenty to enjoy here including swings and slides for children and there are several information boards detailing the history and development of the park. How much of the park you are able to enjoy will depend on the amount of time available before you commence your return to Gateshead Metro Station. However, you might like to walk in a clockwise direction and finish your visit by the lake. (To visit Saltwell Towers, with its café and visitors' gallery, bear left and find your way to a secluded spot in the centre of the 55 acre park). To leave the park, follow the path around the lake in a clockwise direction and bear left at the end of the lake (you entered the park a couple of hundred yards above on your right) to exit onto West Park Road. **D**

Turn right and follow the path a short distance. Cross over the road with care, turn left and then almost immediately right into Rectory Road. Now continue ahead between the terraced houses, one of several rows of houses down to the River Teams. After about 500 yards, you need to take care when crossing over Whitehall Road. On the right, after a further 200 yards or so, at Windermere Street West, you pass a more modern block of dwellings, part of the internationally renowned Gateshead Talmudical College, and in a short distance, at Bewick Road, you pass the synagogue. Continue for a few hundred yards until the pavement arrives at a main road (Bensham Road). **E**

Cross over the road at the traffic lights to a church, turn right and proceed up the hill. You may be able to catch some fine glimpses of the River Tyne over to your left. After several hundred yards you reach the top of the hill at the aptly named Village Heights. After crossing over the junction with Coatsworth Road, and just past The Crown pub on your right, bear left to follow the signs "Bensham Cycleway: Gateshead M: Town Centre". Just beyond the Borough Arms turn left to enter Windmill Hills Town Park from which you can take advantage of the views of the Newcastle skyline. **F**

Exit from the park past the statue of George Hawks. Continue down the minor road a short distance and as it bears left past Windmill Care Homes, bear right to cross the busy main road at the pedestrian lights. Walk down Walker Terrace past the fine mid-19th century housing on your right. At the end of the road turn left to return to Gateshead Metro Station and the end of the walk.

Saltwell Park & Saltwell Towers

↱ **ROUTE** – Descends to the River Tyne then parallels the river through a pleasant riverside park before passing the educationally oriented Bill Quay Farm and climbing up to Pelaw

🚶 **TERRAIN** – On metalled and surfaced paths with a section on a grassy path that can be avoided. Two or three steep sections

🎩 **REFRESHMENTS** – Pubs, near Hebburn Metro station and at Bill Quay, café (restricted opening) at Bill Quay Farm

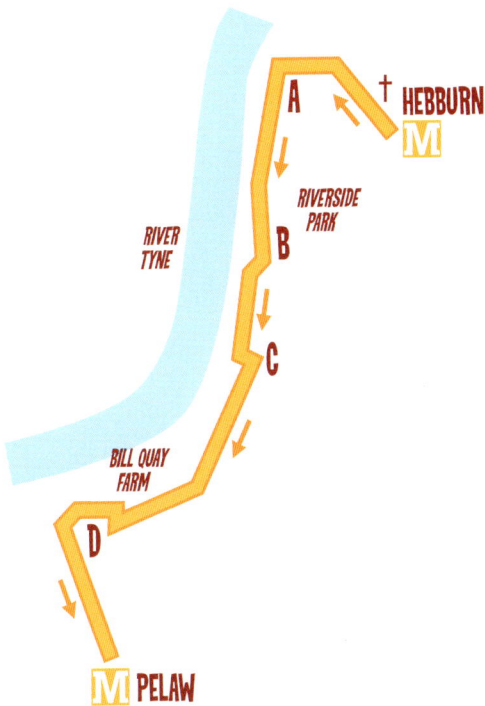

A
† **HEBBURN**
Ⓜ

RIVERSIDE PARK

RIVER TYNE

B

C

BILL QUAY FARM

D

Ⓜ **PELAW**

On exiting from Hebburn Metro Station turn left from Platform 1, or turn right if exiting from Platform 2. Follow the main road (Prince Consort Road) passing Martha's Vineyard pub and St Aloysius RC Church (1888) on your right. At the roundabout bear left in the direction of Prince Consort Industrial Estate, noting, beyond the houses on your right, the fine spire of what was once St Andrew's Church (now used for industrial purposes). Continue ahead as the road makes its way down towards the cranes of the River Tyne. After passing the entrance to the industrial estate, the road bears to the left and levels out. A short distance beyond a small boatyard, take the metalled path on your left, through the waymarked bollards, into the Riverside Park and view the information board. **A**

From here you are walking over a landscape that has been reclaimed from industrial sites, including shipbuilding, chemical and paint works, which once dominated the area. Proceed along the metalled path through the pleasant parkland. You pass some small wooden carvings of symbolic interest: for example, the boat recalls the importance of fishing, shipbuilding and repairing in this area. After about half a mile, at a crossing of paths, you reach a carving of two mushrooms (note, however, that many of the real mushrooms here are poisonous). **B**

Continue ahead for about 60 yards then bear right along a grassy path past a Riverside Nature Trail sign (If the ground is very wet and/or you wish to avoid the grassy section you can continue ahead on the metalled path to point **C**). In a short distance you pass the wooden carving of a horse, horses being used as a way of preserving the local grasslands. The path leads into a plantation and over a short section of boardwalk, near the beginning of which is a carving of a maple leaf. There are good views of the river and across to the opposite bank where suppliers to the off-shore oil industry have largely replaced Tyneside's shipbuilding yards. Continue ahead to find a carving of fish, symbolic of the return of a variety of fish to the decontaminated river. After this carving, the path climbs for a short way to where the path forks. Bear left and climb on the path to meet a metalled path. Turn right and proceed for about 50 yards to reach a metal barrier. **C**

Go straight ahead past the metal barrier onto a surfaced track. Continue along the track and in a short distance you can admire the fine sweep of the River Tyne ahead to your right. The track goes behind some houses on your left and leads onto Brack Terrace. The Bill Quay cricket ground is on your left. Bear right to pass The Wardley pub and arrive at a crossroads. (Down the hill on your right is a further pub, The Cricketers). Continue ahead, crossing the road with care, and walk to the end of Hainingwood Terrace. Turn right and then bear left along the public footpath towards the entrance to the farm buildings of Bill Quay Farm. The farm, containing a good selection of farm animals, is open daily free of charge. There is a café (open on Saturday, Sunday and school holiday afternoons), picnic tables and plenty to see even when the barns are closed (in the mornings). D

To continue the walk, proceed ahead with the farm buildings on your right. Ignore a path off to the right Continue along the path, go through the metal gate and follow the path to Fisherwell Road. Turn left and walk up the hill to meet the main road (Shields Road) at Croxdale Terrace. Cross over the main road with care and walk ahead to Pelaw Metro Station and the end of the walk.

Bill Quay Farm

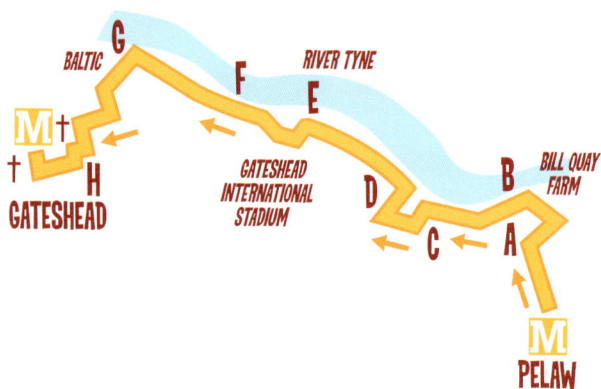

Exit from Pelaw Metro Station and turn left to walk across the bridge over the Metro line. Walk to the road junction at Croxdale Terrace and cross over the busy road with care. Proceed straight ahead down Fisherwell Road. As the road bears to the left at a green area, take the surfaced track on the right that leads between two fences. Go through the metal gate and continue towards the outbuildings of Bill Quay Farm for about 75 yards until you reach a junction of paths. **A** (The entrance to the farm is a short distance beyond this junction. This educationally-oriented project is open daily to the public and offers an interesting collection of livestock and artwork. There is a café with restricted opening on weekends and school holidays).

To continue on the walk, turn sharp left at the junction of paths before the farm buildings. You pass a wooden bench shortly after which the path bears to the right and descends fairly steeply towards the river. The narrow well-trodden path can be slippery in wet weather and care needs to be taken. You soon reach a metalled path on the Keelman's Way. **B**

Turn left and proceed along the path. In a short distance you are walking alongside the River Tyne which is about to sweep towards the right. The skyline of Newcastle comes into view. Continue ahead until you reach a sign "Newcastle Gateshead C2C 14", just beyond the first of a series of industrial buildings belonging to Akzo Nobel, manufacturers of paints and associated products. The route now needs to make a loop around this industrial complex. **C**

Take the path on the left in the direction of the sign and begin to climb away from the river. Turn left onto a minor road at a second C2C sign and continue the gradual climb. After about 200 yards, turn right to pass four metal bollards and continue upwards on a metalled path. As the path levels out, bear right to follow a Keelman's way sign and join a road (Abbotsford Road). Proceed ahead to the end of the road to meet a junction. Turn right and walk downhill to pass the main entrance of the Akzo Nobel complex on your right. Turn left along Nest Road and then turn almost immediately right, just beyond Cromadex, onto a metalled path to continue on the Keelman's Way. **D**

You are now on a pleasant countryside path known as the Friars Goose Riverside Footpath and you soon have the river below on your right. You need to remember, particularly at the narrow sections and bends, that this is a popular route for cyclists. Eventually the path meets a road and you continue ahead for a few yards to a T-junction. Turn right and after about 100 yards you reach an anchor resting on a stone with a plaque that explains the former industrial usages of this area. On your right is the oddly named hotel, bar and bistro the Elephant on the Tyne. **E**

Turn left to meet a stony track which after a short distance arrives at a metalled path. Turn right and follow the path. Ahead you will see the floodlights of Gateshead International Stadium, an important venue for athletics and other sporting events. When the metalled path levels out, take the right-hand fork to join an access road and bear right to return towards the river. Soon you have good views across the river to St Peter's Basin housing complex and marina, while ahead the skyline is somewhat dominated by the massive structure of St James' Park football stadium. When the road turns right to descend to the riverside, bear left to take the metalled path that continues parallel to the river. Eventually you reach an access road and car park area favoured by fishermen. **F**

Cross the road and follow the Cycleway 14 sign to take the narrow surfaced path, past a Keelman's Way sign, through a green area. After a slight incline, the track levels out and broadens opposite the tall white building of a flour mill on the other side of the river, just before you meet a road. Continue ahead along the road that now passes a number of industrial sites and workshops that largely obstruct your view of the river. At a T-junction turn right and then left at Lafarge Redlands Aggregates. Just before you reach the large J Rank Ltd building, now the Baltic Centre for Contemporary Art, turn right and make your way to the riverside. From here you can appreciate the Gateshead Millennium Bridge and the fine buildings of the Newcastle Quayside on the opposite side of the river. You may wish to stop for refreshments and/or visit the art exhibitions at the Baltic. **G**

To continue on the walk, retrace your steps back to the road and follow it as it bears left and climbs away from the river. You pass a modern apartment complex on your right after which you may be able to obtain views of the Sage Music Centre and the Newcastle skyline. Continue uphill until you reach a busy road junction. Cross over the main road by the pedestrian lights and continue ahead up Quarryfield Road. Follow the cyclepath signs and turn right as indicated for the town centre. Walk under the railway bridge and turn left just beyond the entrance to the Davy Roll engineering works. Continue parallel to the busy road and at the end of the wall below the flyover, turn right to descend to a subway signed "To Shopping Centre". Follow the sign to the town centre, passing Park Court on your left and turn left at a minor road. Walk a few yards behind the church and then turn right along Hopper Place to meet a road. On your right is St Edmund's Chapel, the parish church of Gateshead since 1982. The chapel has had a long and interesting history since the first church was built here in mid-13th century. The building has been partitioned off and a large section now houses a local community centre (where details of Trinity Community Association's activities and a history of St Edmund's can be obtained). **H**

Cross over the road at the pedestrian lights and proceed up Jackson Street. Look out on your right for the controversial multi-storey car park that featured in the Michael Caine film *Get Carter* – an argument put forward to prevent its demolition! You arrive at a major junction with St Joseph's RC Church (1859) ahead on the left. Turn right and walk for about 100 yards. Turn left and cross the bus and cycle lanes with care to make your way to Gateshead Metro Station and the end of the walk.

ROUTE – Through Jarrow and along the Rivers Tyne and Don. Then via Bede's World and St Paul's Church to Bede Metro station

TERRAIN – Mainly on the level, on metalled paths and pavements, with one section on a riverside track

REFRESHMENTS – Cafes and pubs in Jarrow and a cafe at Bede's World

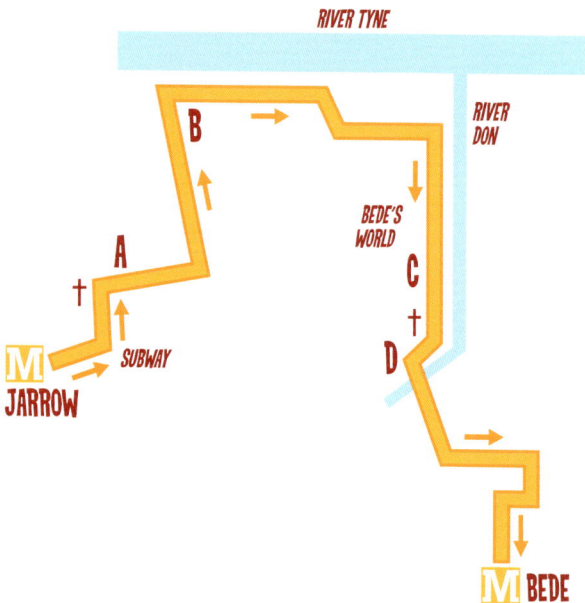

Leave Jarrow Metro Station: from Platform 1, exit via the ramp onto a main road. Before leaving from Platform 2, notice on the left of the platform *The Jarrow March* sculpture by Vince Rae (1984); exit and turn left to walk along Grant Street to arrive, via steps or the ramp, at the main road. Turn left and walk towards the roundabout. Bear left to walk down the paved path. At the bottom, turn right and go through the underpass. Turn left and walk ahead for 150 yards to the crossroads. Over to your left is Christ Church (1868). The sculpture on the right is *The Vikings* by Colin M. Davidson (1962). Walk ahead to cross the road at the traffic island and turn right. Proceed ahead to the red stone and brick council offices, the original Jarrow Town Hall (1902). A plaque commemorates the 1936 Jarrow Crusade against high unemployment. Instead of a loud-voiced campaign, the protesters attempted to convey their message by the quiet dignity of a march by 200 unemployed men from Jarrow to London. **A**

Continue to a T-junction. Turn left and walk along Ferry Street, towards a tunnel ventilation chimney. At the T-junction, cross the road, turn right and walk a few yards and bear left, then immediately left again, at the old-fashioned street light. Proceed along the path through Jarrow Riverside Park. Turn left at the red brick road and walk a few yards, then turn right and go down the ramp. The entrance to the Tyne Pedestrian and Cycle Tunnel is on your left. Continue ahead to the riverside. **B**

Turn right and proceed along the riverside path. Above, on the right, is a statue of Sir Charles Palmer (1822 - 1907), the eminent Victorian shipbuilder whose yards provided employment in Jarrow from 1852 to 1933. Follow the metalled path as it ascends between metal railings. Exit onto a road via a metal gate and turn left. Walk ahead for 150 yards and turn left at the sign "South Shields, River Don Cycleway". Proceed ahead. You pass, on your right, a Celtic-style cross and the path descends to meet a road. Cross the road and bear right to walk along the narrow path running alongside the Don. When the path joins a metalled road, carry on for a few yards to come to steps on the right-hand side. **C**

(A detour up the steps, signposted to Jarrow Museum, is well worthwhile. Here you enter the place where the Venerable Bede (c673-735), monk and historian, lived and worked. The site of his monastery is over to the left, behind St Paul's Church, which has 7th-century foundations and a Saxon chancel. On the right is Bede's World. This features an Anglo-Saxon farm, with animals and crops, and includes Jarrow Hall (1785) which has displays of Anglo-Saxon material and a cafe).

To resume the walk from the foot of the steps, continue in the same direction as before and carry on past the boulders to come to Jarrow Bridge. An information board outlines its history. Go onto the path to the right of the river, passing the ruins of the monastery on your right. Continue ahead and then go up the short flight of steps to a main road (you can avoid the steps by turning right to walk up the ramp). **D**

Turn left and walk down to the junction with a busy road. Follow the pavement round to the left and proceed ahead, passing the Allison Arms on your right and then the Alkali pub on your left, until you reach traffic lights. Turn right to cross the road, then turn left to walk a few yards and turn right. Proceed ahead. At the T-junction turn right, walk a short distance and take the next road on the left. Walk ahead, past the Barbour Factory Outlet Shop, to Bede Metro Station and the end of the walk.

➤ **ROUTE** – To Bede's World, then following pleasant paths along the River Don, via a nature reserve, to Fellgate

🚶 **TERRAIN** – Mostly along metalled paths with some gentle undulation

☕ **REFRESHMENTS** – Two pubs near the start, a cafe at Bede's World and a pub/restaurant on the route

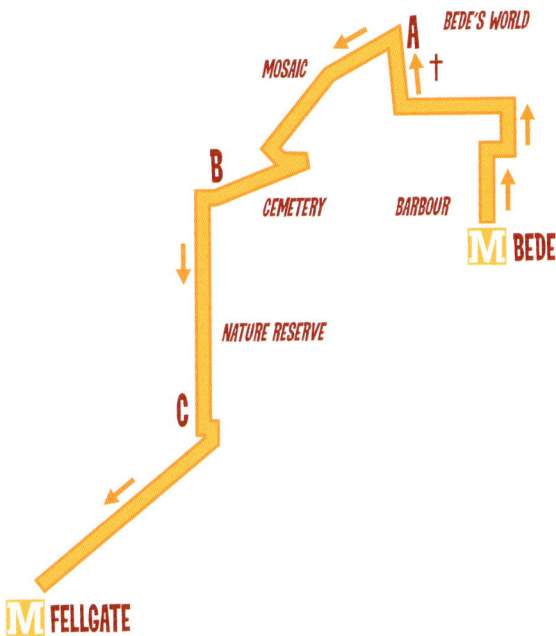

BEDE'S WORLD

MOSAIC

A

†

B

CEMETERY   *BARBOUR*

Ⓜ **BEDE**

NATURE RESERVE

C

Ⓜ **FELLGATE**

Leave Bede Metro Station: from Platform 1, turn left; from Platform 2, turn right. Walk ahead, pass (or visit) the Barbour Factory Outlet Shop. At the T-junction, turn right, walk ahead and turn into the next road on the left. Proceed to the junction at the entrance to the Port of Tyne and cross the road at the traffic lights. Turn left and walk ahead, passing the Alkali pub on your right and the Allison Arms on the left, to come to a road to the right. Follow the pavement as it bears right. Where the pavement ends, cross the road with care and continue in the same direction for about 400 yards to come to a sign on your left for the River Don cycleway. **A**

The walk continues by going onto the cycleway but, time permitting, you may wish to visit the attractions on the other side of the road. This is the place where the Venerable Bede (c673-735) lived and worked. The site of his monastery is behind St Paul's Church, which has 7th-century foundations and a Saxon chancel. Higher up the road is Bede's World. This features an Anglo-Saxon farm, with animals and crops, and includes Jarrow Hall (1785) which has displays and a cafe. To continue the walk, proceed along the cycleway. At a mosaic, take the middle path and continue, going under the road bridge, until you exit from the path at a dual carriageway. Turn left and go under the Metro bridge. After a few yards turn left at a sign for "Primrose". After 100 yards turn right along the path that goes under the road (A19). Turn left near a footbridge and keep on the path, with Jarrow Cemetery on your left, until you arrive at a road. **B**

Cross the road, turn right and walk a few yards, then turn left at a cycleway sign for "Primrose". Proceed along the metalled path and at a T-junction turn left to go over a footbridge. Continue along the path, with the river on your right, to another footbridge. Cross the bridge and carry on, with the river now on your left. You pass picnic tables and viewing platforms at the Primrose Nature Reserve. Follow the path, passing two footbridges. At the end of the cycleway, turn left and walk a few yards to a road. **C**

(If you are ready for a refreshment stop, the Robin Hood, home of the Jarrow Brewery, is nearby). To continue the walk, turn right to cross the road and go under the road bridge. Take the path on the right and after 20 yards bear right. Walk ahead and, about 20 yards before the houses, bear right. Walk to a junction of paths and take the path going down to the right. Bear right at the next junction and then after 50 yards turn left. Proceed ahead with a burn and hedgerow on your left. The path arrives at a main road. Cross the road to the continuation of the path and proceed to Fellgate Metro Station and the end of the walk.

St Paul's Church

ROUTE – Follows the disused West Harton Mineral Line for a while, goes through the extensive recreational spaces of Temple Park and visits the Tilesheds Nature Reserve

TERRAIN – On the level, on metalled paths and surfaced tracks

REFRESHMENTS – Pub near Tyne Dock Metro Station, cafeteria at Temple Park Leisure Centre, pub en route and pub next to East Boldon Metro Station

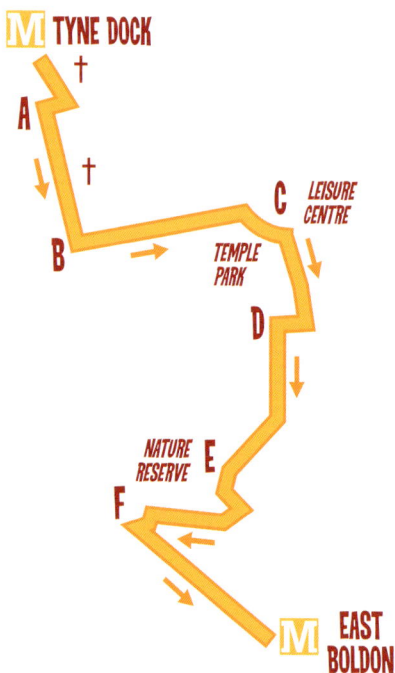

Exiting Tyne Dock Metro Station from Platform 1, turn left and follow the path down the ramp to the main road. Exiting from Platform 2, turn left down the ramp and then after a few yards turn right to follow the path down to the main road. At the main road, turn left and proceed ahead past St Peter and St Paul RC Church (1906) to the traffic lights. Cross over to Barclays Bank, continue ahead to the pedestrian lights. Cross over the road, turn left and walk to Stanley Street with the Colliery Hotel on the corner. Turn right and continue past All

Saints Community Centre to the road end. Go down the short flight of steps and turn left onto the metalled track, formerly the West Harton Mineral Line (alternatively you can join the track via a ramp). Immediately on your left is a small stone carving *Blackberry*. This sculpture is one of a number that you might encounter on this walk that were developed by schoolchildren and groups in conjunction with local artists for the Forest of Imagination Sculpture Trail. **A**

Proceed along the track between the houses. After about 150 yards, at a crossing of paths, you will see All Saints Church (1887-90) over to your left. Continue ahead until you reach a road. Cross with care and pass through the metal barriers noting the linked metal sculpture. Walk along the track and just beyond a road bridge, you reach a sign "Temple Park Leisure Centre". **B**

Turn left, walk through the metal barriers and then pass some houses on your right, to reach the B1298. Cross the road with care at the traffic island, on your right, turn left and then almost immediately right, to enter the park. Immediately on your right is the stone carving *Nuts of Hazel*. Now proceed ahead on the metalled path through the park, keeping roughly parallel to a main road over to your left and ignoring paths off to the right and left. Eventually you will see ahead a large building with an emblem on the top left corner, this is your next destination, Temple Park Centre. The path winds its way forward passing a brick building (Community Safety Centre – Fire Brigade). Then just before the path reaches a main road, take the second of two paths on your right and head towards the leisure centre, its emblem of a crouching figure now clearly visible. After about 400 yards, at a crossing of paths, turn left and follow the path as it snakes its way round to the main entrance of the Temple Park Centre with its leisure facilities and cafeteria. Opposite the entrance are two useful information boards. **C**

To continue, retrace your steps for about 75 yards, bear left just beyond a ringed marker post and follow the path with its lamp posts. You pass a stone carving *Acorn* on your right, before the path winds behind the enclosed football pitch. Just beyond the base of a broken lamp post, take the right-hand fork. Follow the path as it runs roughly parallel to the dual carriageway on your left. At a junction of paths, at the stone carving *Leaf of Oak*, turn left and exit at the dual carriageway (King George Road). Turn right and continue along the pavement with the White Ensign pub on the left-hand side.

At the roundabout, turn right down Nevinson Avenue. On your left, you pass King George V School and the tall *Totem Pole*. Continue ahead and cross the road at the sign "Tilesheds Nature Reserve Brockley Whins". **D**

Proceed in the direction of the cycleway signs down Holder House Way. The school and playing fields are on your left, beyond which you should be able to see the ornate Water Tower (1860-2), with the base of Cleadon Windmill some way to the right. At the end of the road, you pass the entrance to some allotments on your right. Continue ahead between the bollards on a surfaced track. Just after a single wooden gatepost on your right, follow the track as it bears right between wire fences. You pass a large stone and you need to turn round to appreciate the features of the sculpture, the *Green Man*. Continue ahead to pass a wooden barrier at the rear of some houses and after about 200 yards you reach a further stone carving, *Leaf of Beech*. **E**

Turn left and proceed ahead looking out for the wooden sculpture *Whale and Snail* on your right. Then, after a further 75 yards, take the left fork to go through another barrier. At the next fork go right and continue ahead to arrive (and rest ?) at the sculpture *Flowering Seat*, just before a car park. Turn right and continue along the track, parallel to the road beyond the hedgerow on your left, to reach an information board with details of the Tilesheds Nature Reserve and the surrounding area. Go through the metal gate and onto the observation platform to appreciate the small pond, reed beds and wildlife. **F**

To continue on the walk, leave the nature reserve by a second metal gate. Cross the busy road (Tilesheds Lane) with care, turn right and proceed ahead. About 50 yards before the level crossing, turn left to pass in front of some cottages. Carry on in the same direction to follow the path with the Metro track on your right. You pass an interesting collection of small holdings including "The Funny Farm" before you reach Sleepers pub, East Boldon Metro Station and the end of the walk.

ROUTE - From the centre of South Shields, through South Marine Park and then along a pleasant coastal path to Seaburn

TERRAIN - Mainly on surfaced paths with some sections on grassland

REFRESHMENTS - A variety of possibilities at South Shields, Marsden Grotto, Souter Lighthouse and Seaburn

Exit from South Shields Metro Station by following the signs "Seaside (Walking route 10-15 minutes)". Turn right and walk along the pedestrianised King Street. Here you can have refreshments before embarking on the walk and/or if time allows visit the Museum and Art Gallery where you can obtain tourist information and learn about the renowned writer Catherine Cookson. Continue straight ahead following the sign "The Coast A183" along Ocean Road where you will pass an amazing collection of restaurants and takeaways. Just past the public house, The Marine, turn right into South Marine Park. Take the middle of the three paths and follow the yellow line that leads you past the boating lake. After Toney Minchella's ice cream stall, bear right to exit from the park. Cross over the main road in the direction of the sea and walk towards the sea front to the promenade. **A**

Turn right in the direction "Sunderland/Souter Lighthouse". Continue ahead for about a mile until the metalled promenade ends near Trow Point at a National Trust sign. **B**

Turn left, and then, after a few yards, turn right to follow the signs "Coastal footpath" and "Souter Lighthouse 2 miles". From here to the lighthouse the clear path follows the coastline near the protective metal barrier and you can stop from time to time to admire the views and read the interesting information boards. After about 1 mile from Trow Point you reach Marsden Bay with its noted rock (somewhat depleted by erosion in recent years) and the Grotto pub and restaurant. **C**

For the next half-mile or so, the walk continues across the grass to reach Souter Lighthouse. The lighthouse (1871), now under the auspices of the National Trust, is open to visitors from the beginning of April until the end of October and offers a tearoom in addition to a tour and exhibition. **D**

To continue on the walk, keep on the main coastal path for a further mile until you reach the Military Firing Range. (If the range is in use you will be diverted to the main road where you need to turn left. Then proceed until you reach a lane on the left at a dental surgery opposite the cemetery. Turn left and make your way back to the coastal path and resume your journey with the sea on your left. This diversion, if needed, will add about a mile to the walk). Proceed along the coastal path until it ends some 2.5 miles beyond Souter Lighthouse at a road. Follow the road as it bears left and at the City of Sunderland sign turn left to go behind the houses and onto the promenade. Now proceed along the promenade until you arrive opposite the Marriott Hotel on your right. **E**

Turn right to cross the road near the ornamental roundabout, walk past the hotel entrance and bear left up Sea Lane away from the sea front. At the roundabout, turn right and continue uphill (on Chichester Road). As the road levels off and straightens out you come to a shopping area and will see Fulwell Windmill ahead. Continue in the same direction to Seaburn

Metro Station and the end of the walk.

Souter Lighthouse

➜ **ROUTE** - Through South Shields, taking in a variety of contrasting aspects of the town and with river and sea views

🚶 **TERRAIN** - Mainly on pavements and on the level, with a few ascents and descents

☕ **REFRESHMENTS** - A variety of possibilities in South Shields and on the sea front

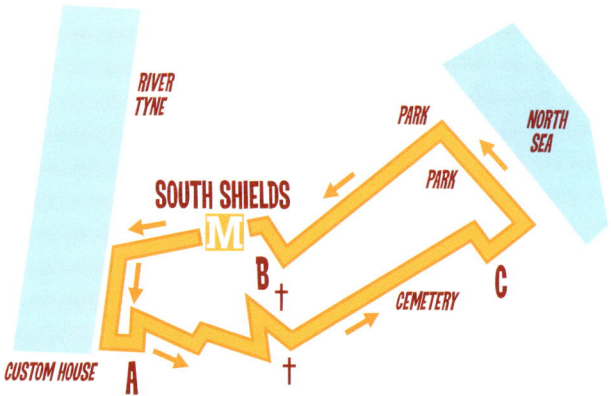

Exit from the South Shields Metro Station by following the signs "Seaside (Walking route 10-15 minutes)" as far as the exit. At the exit turn left and walk along the pedestrianised street (King Street) to reach Market Square. Over to the left is the mainly 18th-century St Hilda's Church. Go straight ahead, through the arches of the Old Town Hall (1768) and through arches in the building opposite, and descend to a road. Turn left and walk a few yards, then turn right to cross the road at the traffic island. Go down the metalled path towards the river to arrive at a promenade on the regenerated riverside. The pedestrian ferry terminal is ahead. You might also see one of the large passenger ships sailing majestically to or from the North Shields terminal. Turn left where immediately on your left you will find an information panel about ferries and tugs. Proceed ahead until you arrive at the Merchant Navy Memorial (1990) behind which is a plaque in tribute to Jim Slater, former General Secretary of the National Union of Seamen. Turn left to pass The Customs House on your right. The building has been restored and operates as a thriving arts centre. **A**

Walk ahead for about 100 yards to the second junction and turn left. Proceed uphill passing a number of pubs on the opposite side. At the top of the bank, turn right and, with care, cross the road at the traffic island. Bear left and walk uphill. Over the road on your left there is a metal wheel representing the mining industry, once a very important part of the local economy. Use another traffic island, just beyond Secretan Way, to cross to the other side and carry on in the same direction. Turn left into Henry Robson Way. On the left you come to the restored Pump House of the former St Hilda Colliery together with an information panel giving details of its history. Walk to the end of the road and turn right onto the pedestrian/cycleway to "Sunderland, Souter Lighthouse and Sea Front". Continue straight ahead and exit to a road via metal barriers. Turn left and walk ahead. At the junction with the statue of Queen Victoria ahead turn right and use the traffic lights to cross the road. Turn left and walk a few yards to reach the corner. **B**

The building opposite is South Shields Town Hall (1905). Now, turn right and proceed along the road (Westoe Road). On the left you pass Westoe Baptist Church (1881), and on the right St Bede's Catholic Church (1876). About 60 yards past the church cross the road at the traffic island, bear left and enter the pedestrian/cycleway signposted "Sunderland, Souter Lighthouse and Sea Front". Proceed ahead, eventually passing a cemetery on your right. Carry on to come to a road. Cross the road and continue in the same direction to a T-junction. Turn right and after a few yards cross the road and enter the grassy area (Bents Recreation Ground). **C**

Beyond the recreation ground over to the right is The Leas, finishing point of the Great North Run. You might want to avoid doing the walk on the day of the race! Rain or shine, the whole area will be busy as, apart from the many spectators, around 40,000 runners usually take part. Proceed ahead towards the sea and exit the recreation ground. Turn left and walk along the brightly-coloured, wide pavement. Ahead in the distance, weather permitting, you can enjoy a good view of Tynemouth Priory and Castle. You pass a caravan site and a park (Bents Park). At the end of the pavement, proceed ahead crossing the road with care to enter the park (South Marine Park). Bear left to pass between the ice cream outlet and the boating lake. Bear left to ascend by the path parallel to the road on the left. Exit from the park via the gates on the left, cross Seaview Terrace (ignoring a sign to the Metro) and walk up Beach Road. Continue in the same direction heading towards the Town Hall in the distance. Before the Town Hall, at a mini roundabout, turn right and walk down Anderson Street. Continue ahead, using the steps or the ramp, until you reach the roundabout at Asda. Turn left to cross the road with care and walk ahead with Asda on your right. On the left you pass the Museum and Art Gallery where you can obtain tourist information and learn about the renowned writer Catherine Cookson. Continue in the same direction to South Shields Metro Station and the end of the walk.

ROUTE – Through Exhibition Park, across the Town Moor and finish via Leazes Park

TERRAIN – Mainly on the level on pavements and metalled paths with one short, steep ascent. There are several short flights of steps (alternative route indicated)

REFRESHMENTS – In Spital Tongues and Newcastle centre

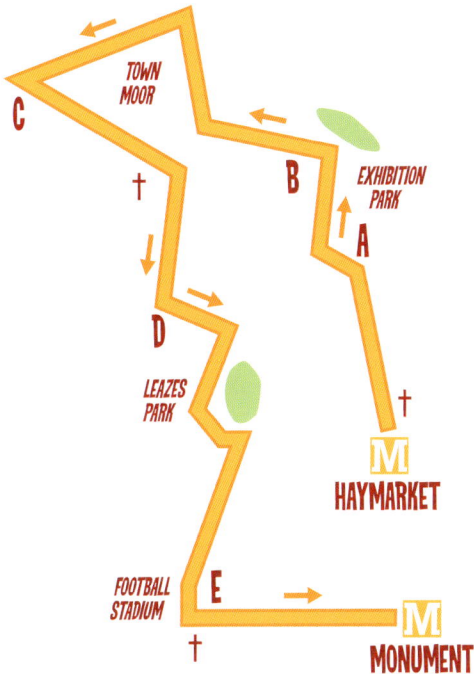

TOWN MOOR

C

B   EXHIBITION PARK

A

†

D

LEAZES PARK

M
HAYMARKET

FOOTBALL STADIUM   E

†   M
MONUMENT

From the top of the escalator, walk to the left to exit from the Haymarket Metro Station. Immediately on your left is the South African (Boer) War Memorial, depicting the goddess Victory. Cross the road at the traffic lights and walk ahead on the main pavement with St Thomas's Church on your right. St Thomas's Church (1825-1830) was designed by John Dobson (1787-1865), the famous Newcastle architect. There are three further war memorials outside the church. The new glass gates symbolise "linking of the church with the world". Walk ahead and turn left to cross by the traffic lights to join Kings Walk.

(To avoid flights of steps on the next section, turn right and walk to the junction. Turn left and walk up Claremont Road to a set of pedestrian lights. Now follow directions from **A**). Proceed ahead through the grounds of the University of Newcastle. Go through the arches. On your left is the Museum of Archaeology and, over to the right, the Hatton Gallery. Admission to both is free. Walk through the quadrangle. At the top go down the steps on the right and at the bottom of the second flight of steps bear right and walk to the road ahead. Turn left and walk a few yards to pedestrian lights. **A**

Cross the road at the lights. Turn left and proceed to the roundabout ahead and the entrance to Exhibition Park. The park acquired its name when the former recreation ground there was redesigned for the North East Coast Exhibition of 1929 (Scottish and Newcastle Breweries' Exhibition Ale appeared at the same time). Walk into the park. Take care because park vehicles use this route. Follow the road, passing a cafe on your right, to arrive at the lake. The walk continues to the left but you may, first, wish to visit the Military Vehicle Museum on the opposite side. To continue the walk, turn left and proceed to a wide gate and exit the park onto the Town Moor. This vast green expanse is sometimes referred to as "Newcastle's lung". It is owned by the city for the benefit of Newcastle townsfolk who have free access but the grazing rights belong to the city's Freemen. **B**

Walk ahead and at the junction of paths turn right. At the next junction turn right onto the path with the street lights. Walk ahead to the crossing of paths and turn left. Proceed on this path to a bridge over the dual carriageway. The mounds ahead over to the right (formed from the excavated waste when the road was built) are the highest points around and provide views over to the Cheviot Hills. Cross the bridge and turn left to exit the Town Moor at a road junction. **C**

Cross to the other side of Claremont Road. This area is the peculiarly-named Spital Tongues, formerly a small colliery village. Turn left and walk down the road, passing the remains of a windmill and St Luke the Evangelist's Church (1886), and turn right into North Terrace at The North Terrace pub. At the end of the street go straight ahead and proceed along the footpath which runs between university buildings. Exit onto a busy road and, with care, cross to the other side. **D**

Turn left and proceed down the road. The Royal Victoria

Infirmary is on the left and Leazes Park is on the right. The park was created in 1873 as Newcastle's first public park and has recently undergone an extensive restoration scheme to bring it back to its Victorian splendour. A short distance after the traffic island, go into the park and immediately turn left. After a few yards, turn right to arrive at the side of the lake. Turn right and enjoy a walk round the lake. Just before the end of the lake, when you are more or less in line with the infirmary chimney, turn right and walk ahead. To your right a tree trunk has been transformed into a sculpture. Carry on and exit the park where the stadium and the splendid early 19th-century terrace of houses almost meet. Turn left and walk along two sides of Leazes Terrace. At the T-junction, turn right and walk a few yards to St James Street. Turn left and walk to the end of the road. Cross at the pedestrian lights and turn right to come to The Strawberry pub. At the corner, turn left and walk by the side of the pub. Look for the board outlining the pub's history and the derivation of its name. St James' Park, home of Newcastle United, and St James Metro Station are over to your right. **E**

Proceed down the street (Strawberry Lane). At the end, opposite St Andrew's Church, turn left. Walk ahead over the busy crossroads to pass Eldon Square on your left and arrive at Grey's Monument, Monument Metro Station and the end of the walk.

Grey's Monument

Monument to Central Station (3 miles)

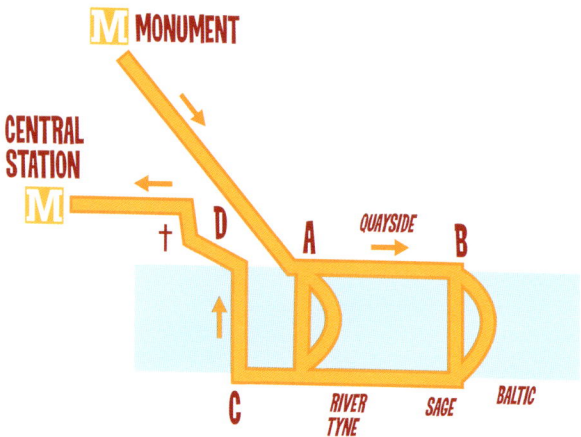

Leave Monument Metro Station by the Theatre Royal exit which takes you to the top of Grey Street. This street, designed by the builder and entrepreneur Richard Grainger (1797-1861), is generally acknowledged to be one of the most elegant streets in Newcastle. On the right is an entrance to the attractively designed Central Arcade (1906), while behind the Metro Station stands Grey's Monument, a tribute to Earl Grey who was largely responsible for the Parliamentary Reform Act of 1832. Proceed ahead to cross Market Street, after which you will see the classically colonnaded Theatre Royal (1836-37) on your left. Continue descending, taking time to admire the many fine buildings. Cross over Mosley Street at the traffic lights and proceed ahead down Dean Street, with its splendid variety of buildings including, on the left, some brick houses (now shops) of the late 18th century and, on the right, the colourful Cathedral Buildings. Follow the road as it bears left and then right into Sandhill. Ahead to the right is the Guildhall, a frequently remodelled building, owing its origins to the merchants' hall and town court of at least the 16th century. Make your way towards the River Tyne to arrive beneath the towering structure of the Tyne Bridge (1925-28). **A**

Turn left and proceed, with the River Tyne on your right, along the Quayside, the location of a popular Sunday market. On the opposite side of the river is the Tuxedo Princess, a floating night club. On your left you will see a fine collection of buildings, several, as indicated by wall plaques, formerly part of the Tyne's once thriving shipping trade. On your left, after about 200 yards, are the Law Courts, a newer edition to the Quayside (1984-90). On your right you reach the Millennium Bridge, officially opened by H.M The Queen during her Jubilee Tour in May 2002. This modern "eye" tilts to allow vessels to pass underneath and a timetable shows when this generally occurs. **B**

Cross the bridge into Baltic Square with the Baltic Centre for Contemporary Art, formerly a 1950's grain warehouse, on the left hand-side. Here you can pay a visit to see the exhibitions, to obtain some splendid views of the River Tyne and /or to enjoy some refreshments. To continue on the walk, leave Baltic Square by the steps or the ramp to meet a road. Turn right and proceed ahead with the river now on your right. A sign indicates that you are heading in the direction of Wylam and Rowlands Gill on the Keelman's Way (a 14 mile route from Wylam to Bill Quay). On your left you soon pass the futuristic-looking Sage Music Centre, while on your right you get a closer look at the Tuxedo Princess before walking beneath the Tyne Bridge again. You arrive at some traffic lights, just over 100 yards to the left of which is Gateshead Quays Visitor Centre, formerly St Mary's Church. Here you can learn about the development of the area. To continue on the walk, turn right at the traffic lights and almost immediately left at another set of lights and descend to the Port of Tyne's Swing Bridge, a major engineering achievement of 1868-76 by William Armstrong's company. **C**

Cross over the bridge and at the far end on the left-hand side you will see the Fish Market building (1880), now a night-spot like so many of these fine old buildings. Follow the pavement to the pedestrian lights and cross over the road. Turn right and after a few yards, turn left after Mansion House Chambers to climb the Castle Stairs. (Alternatively, to avoid the steep steps, continue ahead and retrace your steps to the bottom of Dean Street. Bear left at Milburn House to go up the Side and reach the Cathedral Church of St Nicholas. Now follow the route from **D** below). The steps lead into an area known as the Castle Garth. Ahead is the Castle Keep (1168-1178). To the right is the Moot Hall (1810-12), formerly a county court and prison and now the Crown Court, and the Vermont Hotel (formerly the offices of Northumberland County Council). Over to the left is the Bridge Hotel. Continue ahead passing the Keep on your left to go under the railway bridge. Bear right to cross the wooden ramp that goes through the Black Gate, a gatehouse named after Patrick Black a 17th-century tenant. Turn right and walk about 100 yards to arrive at the Cathedral Church of St Nicholas, a parish church of the 14th century which became the Anglican cathedral in 1882, the year Newcastle became a city and the Diocese of Newcastle was formed out of the Durham Diocese. **D**

At the traffic lights turn left and proceed along Collingwood Street. Cross over the road at the lights and turn right. To your right you will see the monument of 1862 by John Lough to George Stephenson, the noted railway engineer, appropriately located near to the Central Station to where you now proceed to the Metro Station and the end of the walk.

Baltic & Millennium Bridge

➜ **ROUTE** - Through part of the centre of Newcastle and on to the quayside. Then along the riverside before ascending to Byker. The route passes a number of historical buildings as well as a contrasting mix of domestic architectural styles

🚶 **TERRAIN** - Mostly on pavements and on the level. However, there are some steep ascents and descents, sometimes via steps

☕ **REFRESHMENTS** - A variety of possibilities throughout the walk

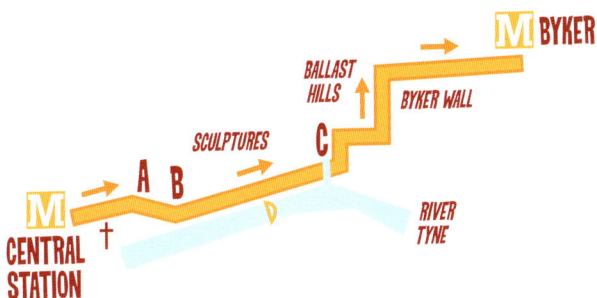

Leave the Metro Station by the Neville Street exit. Walk ahead passing the Royal Station Hotel on your right. On the left is the George Stephenson Monument (1862), the noted railway engineer, by the distinguished sculptor John Lough (1798-1876). Cross Orchard Street. Bear left and use the pedestrian lights to cross Westgate Road. and carry on in the same direction along Collingwood Street. Continue with care over the next junction. You pass St Nicholas' Cathedral on your right. Cross Dean Street and continue to the road intersection. Use the traffic lights to cross over to Bar 55. Bear right and walk around the building to the entrance to an underpass. Go through the underpass to the red-brick Holy Jesus Hospital (1681), a former almshouse, now administered by the National Trust. It houses an exhibition which is open on Monday – Friday afternoons (not Bank Holidays) and there is a full tour on the first Saturday of each month (February – December). **A**

After looking at the hospital, retrace your steps back to the underpass, then turn left and proceed in the direction "Cuthbert House". Carry on, following the directions to "Aidan House

(Tax Office)". You pass through arches of the railway bridge. At the end of the blue railings turn left, cross the road, turn left and proceed downhill. Above on your left (up Croft Stairs), are the remains of the unusual corner tower, built when the town wall was extended to embrace a new area. Bear right and proceed across the pedestrian zone, passing the One Trinity building on your left. Carry on. On the right is Trinity House (much rebuilt in 1841), a medieval foundation whose main responsibilities relate to navigation and lighthouses. If it is open, the courtyard is well worth a visit. At the junction with the quayside turn left, cross to the new building on the corner (Law Courts) then immediately turn right to cross via traffic lights to the riverside path. **B**

Turn left and proceed in the direction "Hadrian's Way", with the River Tyne on your right. Continue ahead, passing the Millennium Bridge and a series of modern sculptures. On your left you pass the Malmaison Hotel which has retained part of the façade of the original Cooperative Society building. Continue straight on to the apartment blocks ahead. Follow the path in front of the Mariners' Wharf apartments with a fish sculpture on your right. Turn left at the end of the last block and after a few yards turn right in the direction "National Cycleway Network 72". Immediately after crossing a road bridge turn left to cross the road with care and go to the right of The Tyne Bar. Bear right, just before the arch of the Glasshouse Bridge (1878), a reminder of one-time significance of glassworks in this area, and go up the steep steps. At the top walk ahead for a few yards then turn left to cross the road with care. Turn into Albion Row and walk ahead. On your left is the entrance to the little park of Ballast Hills. A plaque outlines its interesting history and provides details of its "unique but fragile pathway". **C**

Proceed up Albion Row for about 100 yards and turn right to walk along St Michael's Road. You pass a park on your right (St Lawrence Park). Just after the park turn into the road on your left (Dalton Street) and proceed ahead. The road skirts the famous Byker Wall housing development. Bear to the right along Conyers Road and walk to Byker Metro Station and the end of the walk.

ROUTE - Goes through the architecturally famous Byker Wall and then proceeds along the banks of the River Tyne to arrive at the Segedunum Roman fort, baths and museum close to the shipyards at Wallsend

TERRAIN - On surfaced tracks and almost entirely on the level apart from the initial descent to the river and one steady climb. There is a short flight of steps that can be avoided

REFRESHMENTS - Pub at St Peter's Basin and one close to Swan Hunter shipyard; cafe at Segedunum Museum

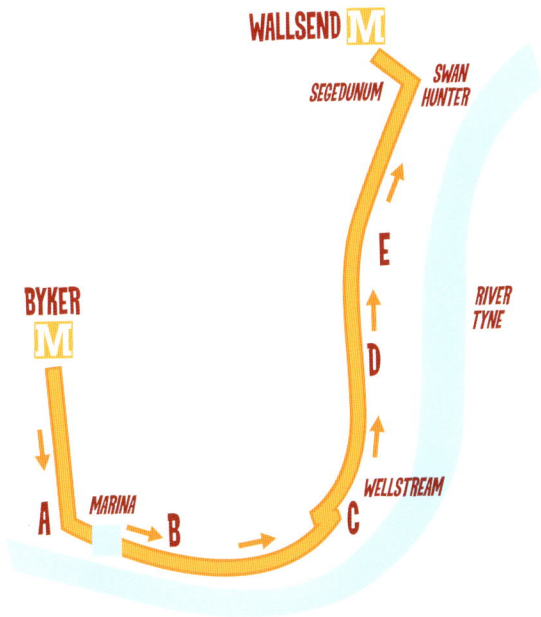

WALLSEND M

SWAN HUNTER

SEGEDUNUM

E

BYKER M

RIVER TYNE

D

MARINA

A

B

C

WELLSTREAM

Exit from Byker Metro Station, turn right, cross the road and proceed straight ahead through Rabygate. This is one of the entrances through the "wall" of the Byker redevelopment scheme which sought to revitalise this area of Newcastle. This award - winning design by Ralph Erskine was once considered a model for local authority housing. As you go through the archway you will see some interesting old stones and remnants of pillars. Before proceeding further ahead, you might like to stop and turn round to view some of the green and blue timber balconies and walkways. Continue down Raby Street for a few hundred yards, crossing Commercial Road, with care, to pass through Raby Cross. After a further couple of hundred yards you should get your first glimpse of the River Tyne as you arrive at the A186 (Walker Road). Cross at the traffic lights, continue your descent and cross over St Lawrence Road. About 100 yards from the river, just beyond a car park area, look out, on your right, for a sign for Hadrian's Way. **A**

Turn left to cross the road and walk ahead. Soon you enter an area of modern housing (St Peter's Basin). Turn right, just before the Fog on the Tyne and the marina, in the direction "Hadrian's Way, Lower Route". Walk to the riverside at Chandlers Quay where, almost hidden in the bushes on your left, is the foundation stone laid in 1989 by the then Prime Minister, Mrs Thatcher. As you enjoy your first close look at the river, across the other side, to the right, you should be able to see the floodlights of Gateshead International Stadium. Turn left and continue ahead, crossing the bridge at the Marina Office, and follow the pavement as it continues along the riverside. Soon you pass a Royal Bank of Scotland milepost which indicates on one side that you are on Cycleway 72, and on the other side that you are $9\frac{1}{4}$ miles from the mouth of the Tyne. You then come to the end of the housing and you join a surfaced track. **B**

Proceed along the riverside track. You will find shrubs on your left and, on the opposite side of the river, you will see the Friars Goose marina beside the Elephant on the Tyne. Proceed for several hundred yards. Across the river there is an industrial complex. Ignore a road and paths off to the left as you walk through a popular area from which to fish. (If you wish to avoid the short flight of steps that lies ahead, then you need to divert from the riverside path as you come level with a small industrial complex on the opposite bank of the river and just before the path takes a sharp turn to the left. Climb a short way bearing right, then turn right at a Hadrian's Way sign to descend back to the riverside path near the top of the steps). The riverside path eventually leads you up a flight of six steps, shortly after which you will see ahead Wellstream (suppliers to the oil and gas industry). Before reaching the industrial plant, you arrive at a fork in the path at a brick wall with seating spaces. **C**

Fork left, in the direction "Hadrian's Way Wallsend", to leave the riverside path and follow the path as it zig-zags up the bankside for a few hundred yards. It then levels off at a green area with two blue benches commemorating the Millennium. There are good views across the river to Pelaw and Bill Quay. Continue ahead along a pleasant tree-lined section and then pass two yellow cranes at the Duco engineering and cable plant on your right, and then housing on your left. Cross a road with care. After a couple of hundred yards, more cranes appear ahead, a reminder of the former dominance of shipyards on the Tyne. After crossing a bridge, you pass the Wincomblee Workshops on your right. **D**

Continue ahead to follow the signs for Cycleway 72, with evidence from time to time of the fact that you are following the line of an old railway. Cross a road and proceed ahead behind some renovated post-war prefab housing. The path descends to some traffic lights and under the old railway bridge on your right you will see two plaques, reminders of the significance of the Emperor Hadrian to this area as we approach his "wall's end". **E**

Cross the road and continue ahead passing the Swan Hunter shipyard, responsible for building a large number of important passenger and naval ships and oil tankers, but now, since its resurgence from receivership in 1993, employing only a tiny fraction of its once huge workforce. On the left ahead, beyond the bridge, you will soon see the viewing tower of Segedunum, while, some 50 yards beyond the bridge, on the right, dwarfed by the cranes, is The Ship Inn. The whitewashed walls on your left house the replica Roman baths of Segedunum. In a short distance, you cross a bridge with the entrance to Swan Hunter below on your right. After a further 30 yards, turn left to leave the cycleway and follow the path as it makes its way to the access road. Cross the road and walk up to the traffic lights, noting the cast-iron clock, formerly the shipyard clock and sited a little further north. To visit the Segedunum complex, turn left and walk a few yards to the entrance. The museum tells the story from Wallsend's Roman past to its modern industrial heritage. Visitors are welcome to use the cafe and gift shop. To complete the walk, cross over the road (Buddle Street) at the traffic lights. Proceed ahead along Station Road for about 100 yards to Wallsend Metro Station and the end of the walk (don't be confused by the signs in Latin, just make sure you get onto the correct *suggestus* for your return journey!).

Wallsend to Walkergate
(4 miles)

ROUTE - Through an area of Roman heritage before going into the centre of Wallsend. Then via a park and the perimeter of a golf course to Walkergate

TERRAIN - Mostly on pavements and surfaced paths. Mainly on the level but with a few fairly steep ascents and descents, sometimes via steps

REFRESHMENTS - A variety of possibilities in Wallsend, a sports centre bar on route and a pub at the end of the walk

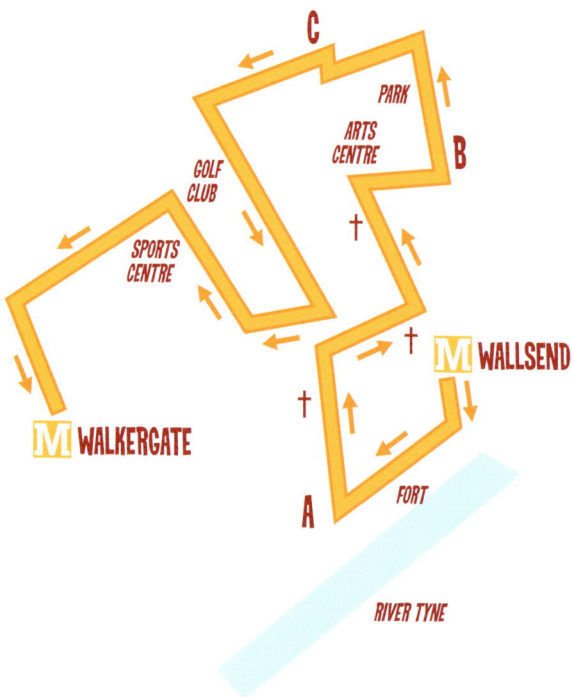

Before leaving Wallsend Metro Station, you will see that several of the notices have been translated into Latin, so as to emphasize the Roman antecedents of this area. Exit the station; from Platform 1(from the steps) turn right, walk ahead for a few yards, then turn right again to go under the Metro bridge; from Platform 2 (from the steps) turn right (the Metro bridge is behind you). Proceed in the direction of the entrance to the Swan Hunter shipyard which is ahead. At the traffic lights cross the road and turn right. Walk ahead to come to the entrance to Segedunum Roman Museum, which is well worth a visit if time permits. Carry straight on. Behind the railings on your left you have a good view of the layout of the foundations of the fort. These lay under streets of terraced housing until they were exposed following the redevelopment of the area several years ago. Further over to the left, the white building is a reconstruction of a Roman bathhouse. Turn right to cross the road at a zebra crossing. Turn left and walk a few yards and go through the gate into the enclosed area. Here there are several interesting features of historical significance, as well as a reconstruction of a section of the Wall. **A**

Leave the site by the same gate. Turn left and walk ahead for 40 yards, then turn left and proceed along Carville Road passing Harry's Bar (1893). Carry on under the Metro line, passing the Catholic Church of Our Lady and Saint Columba (1957) on your left. Turn right and walk along Frank Street. On the left, set into an arcade of the Wallsend Memorial Hall, is a War Memorial to the employees of the Swan Hunter & Wigham Richardson Ltd shipyard, once a mainstay of the local economy. You reach a junction (with Station Road). On the right is St Luke's Church (1887). Over the road, the property now occupied by the Happy Chef was once the family dairy and home of Sting, the international musician and rock star. Sting recalls walking from there every Saturday morning to his music lesson, with his guitar wrapped in a plastic bag to protect it from the rain. Often to be greeted with "Giz a tune on ya banjo bonnie lad" by local people. Turn left and walk ahead, crossing at the traffic lights to arrive at The Anson pub on your left. In front of The Anson is a statue of a woman carrying a basket of hens; this is a representation of a Roman market woman, by Hans Schwartz (1967). A panel on the pub wall gives details of how the pub got its name and the origin of the phrase "penny wet". (Over to the left is The Forum shopping complex which includes a Thornton's coffee shop). Continue in the same direction. You pass Trinity Methodist Church before arriving at traffic lights. Cross North Road and after 40 yards turn right to cross at the pedestrian lights to the Buddle Arts Centre. Turn right, walk a few yards then turn left to walk along North Road. Soon you come to an entrance to Richardson Dees Park. **B**

Go into this attractive park where pleasant walks can be enjoyed. Part of the land for the park was donated by Robert Richardson Dees, a local solicitor and benefactor. Bear right and follow the perimeter path. You pass some sad tennis courts on your left. Go down the steep steps and carry on, alongside a small lake. Then leave the metalled path to continue ahead with a stream on your left. Continue until the stream goes into a culvert, then go up the narrow path on the right and exit the park. Cross the road, turn left and walk a few yards then go onto the path off to the right. Walk ahead, above the little valley. Eventually you will see traffic on a busy road ahead of you (A1058). Take a path off to the left, just after a wooden seat and about 80 yards before you reach the road, and descend to a bridge. Cross over the bridge. Bear right and go up the path via steps to exit onto a pavement on the busy Coast Road. **C**

Turn left and proceed to a roundabout. Continue in the same direction, taking great care as you cross the road. Walk along Devonshire Gardens. Cross Derby Gardens and at the next corner turn left and proceed along West Street. At a convenient point cross to the other side. Wallsend Golf Club is on your right. You pass The Lindisfarne social club on the left and come to crossroads. Turn right and proceed ahead. Turn right into Rheydt Avenue and walk to the Wallsend Sports Centre. (If you require refreshments you need to bear left to the bar/restaurant which is near the far end of the complex on the left). The walk goes straight through the car park to arrive at a vehicle barrier in the right-hand corner. Go past the barrier and bear left along the bridleway. Eventually you reach a road. Cross the road and carry on along the metalled path to a main road (Benfield Road). Turn left and proceed along the road for just over half a mile to Walkergate Metro Station and the end of the walk.(The Railway pub is on the left, just after the Metro station).

Segedunum Roman Museum

ROUTE - Through Howden and the Tyne Pedestrian Tunnel to Jarrow

TERRAIN - Not for the faint-hearted. The walk goes through the tunnel and, because it is much less used than in its heyday, you might be the only pedestrian going through. After a gentle descent the walk is all on the level, on metalled paths and pavements

REFRESHMENTS - A café in Bede's World and several cafés and pubs in Jarrow

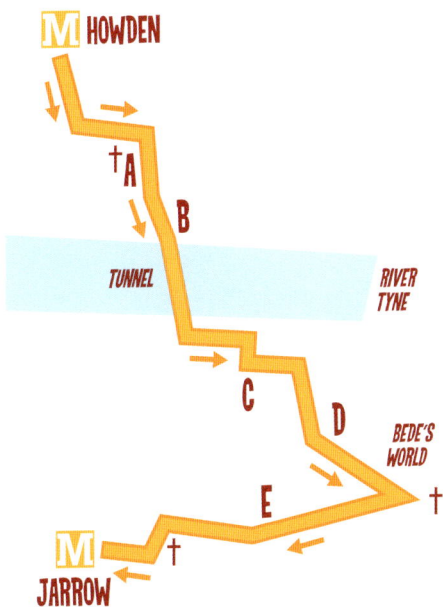

Leave Howden Metro Station: from Platform 1, turn right and then right again to cross the Metro line; from Platform 2, turn left. Walk ahead, passing Howden Park on your left. When the road completes its descent turn left to walk along Norman Terrace. Just past the church, turn right and pass the east end of St Paul's Church, Willington Quay (1876). The absence of a notice board might give the impression that the church is closed. However, at the time of writing, it still is in use for Sunday and other services. **A**

Carry on along the road (Cumberland Street). At the junction, turn left and walk a few yards, then use the traffic island to cross the road with care. Go through the gap in the railings. Bear left and follow the metalled path. The surface becomes cobbled for a short section and exits onto a road. Turn right and walk towards the entrance to the Tyne pedestrian and cycle tunnels. On the right, in the aptly-named Stephenson Street, there is an information board with details of local connections with George Stephenson the railway engineer. Just before the entrance there are two sculptures by Fiona Gray (2004): *The ones that got away* and *The Echo*. At the entrance there is an information panel with details of the tunnel's fascinating history. **B**

Use the escalator (one of the longest in the world at the time of its construction) or, if this is not operating, the lift to enter the tunnel. Go through the tunnel. Its length clearly confirms that you are passing underneath the River Tyne. Near the exit there is an exhibition of photographs about the construction and opening of the tunnel and a panel with technical details. Walk ahead and go up the fairly steep steps to come to a red-brick road. You can see a tunnel ventilation funnel ahead. Turn left and walk ahead to an information panel about "Palmer's town" and details of a local heritage walk, part of which you will be following. The statue some way behind the panel is of Sir Charles Palmer, shipbuilder, whose yards provided employment in Jarrow from 1852 to 1933. Continue in the same direction for a short distance and take the path past the bollard on the right into the park. Keep to the left and bear left just past the circle to exit the park onto a road. **C**

Turn left and proceed along the road (Curlew Road). Follow the road as it bears right. Continue ahead along Priory Road, past the storage tanks of the Shell UK Jarrow Terminal on your left, and turn left into Church Bank. Walk ahead to an information panel about "a special place". **D**

The walk continues in the same direction but a detour to Bede's world is well worthwhile. Bede's World features an Anglo-Saxon farm, with animals and crops, and includes Jarrow Hall (1785) which has a cafe. Continue down the hill (Church Bank) for 200 yards or so to the entrance to the grounds of St Paul's Church. If time permits you can visit the church, which has 7th century foundations and a Saxon chancel, as well as the remains of the monastery which is adjacent on the south side. Here you enter the area where the Venerable Bede (c673-735), monk and historian, lived and worked. Cross the road with care and take the River Don

Cycleway. Follow the path and, at a mosaic, carry straight on. Continue past another mosaic to arrive at a road. **E**

Bear right and cross at the traffic lights. Go onto the broad paved path ahead. In a few yards bear left and follow the path over the green. At the junction with a road, turn left and proceed ahead. The entrance to the vehicular Tyne Tunnel is below on the right. Walk towards the roundabout. Bear left to the end of the railings and cross the road with care at the traffic island. Walk ahead for 20 yards and turn right to cross at another traffic island. Proceed ahead on the broad path and cross the road to arrive at St Bede's Catholic Church (1862). Walk to the right of the church and turn left. Walk ahead and follow the pavement past the Crown and Anchor. Turn right at a junction of paths then almost immediately bear left. Follow the path, past the entrance to an underpass. Turn left and go through the second underpass. Turn immediately left and follow the ramp to Jarrow Metro Station and the end of the walk. In the station there is an information panel with details of local walks embracing places of historical interest. On Platform 2 there is a sculpture *Jarrow Crusade* by Vince Rae (1984) commemorating the famous march to London by 200 unemployed men in 1936.

WALK 36

Percy Main to Shiremoor
(4 miles)

ROUTE – Follows a disused railway line, passes a railway museum, diverts into a park where there is a climb to a splendid viewpoint and then continues on to Shiremoor

TERRAIN – On the level along metalled paths and surfaced tracks with a climb that could be omitted

REFRESHMENTS – Pub at the beginning and near the end of the walk and hotel en route

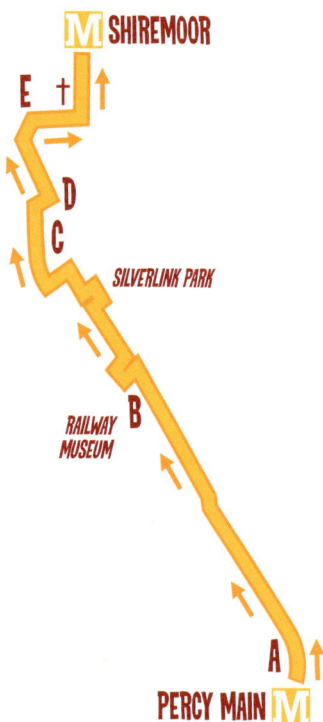

M SHIREMOOR

E †

D

C

SILVERLINK PARK

B

RAILWAY MUSEUM

A

PERCY MAIN M

Exit from Platform 1 to meet a road and turn left, or if exiting from Platform 2 turn right. Follow the road past The Percy Arms and then after about 200 yards, just before the road sign for the roundabout (Tynemouth A1058) turn left to join the metalled path onto the National Cycle Network 10. **A**

Follow the metalled path under two adjacent bridges and proceed straight ahead as the path goes parallel to the North

Tyneside Steam Railway line. The track goes under a main road (Coast Road) and the railway line disappears off towards the left. Ignore paths off until eventually the track meets a main road. Turn left and walk about 100 yards to the entrance to the Stephenson Railway Museum (the museum which contains memorabilia and explanations of the north-east's important railway heritage is open, free of charge, May-September except on Mondays and Fridays). **B**

To continue the walk, from the museum cross the busy road with care, turn right and walk a few yards to take the public footpath "West Allotment 1m 1.5Km". After a few yards, turn right to pass a vehicle barrier and then, after a further 50 yards on the surfaced track, turn left. Continue ahead, passing reed beds and dense hedgerows, as the pleasant track climbs very gently for several hundred yards until you reach a T-junction. Turn right and then left to go through a vehicle barrier and meet a minor road. Cross the road with care and continue ahead on the public bridleway. After a few yards go through a barrier and turn left. Follow the surfaced path as it bears right and arrives at a sign "Silverlink Park biodiversity in North Tyneside". Continue ahead towards the Silverlink Sundial which you will see on the rise. At a major crossing of paths, turn left and follow the path past three small ponds. Bear right at the fork to walk beside a fourth and larger pond. Near the end of this pond you reach a broad surfaced area. On the right a path leads to the sundial which can be reached either by steps or by the longer route on the path. From the top of the rise there are views of Tyneside and far beyond. **C**

To continue on the walk, retrace your steps from the sundial to the broad surfaced area, turn right and continue ahead. After just under 100 yards, take the left-hand fork and proceed parallel to the road on your left until you arrive at a car park. There is an information board on your right and across the road to your left is the Village Hotel (open to visitors for refreshments). Continue ahead, ignoring paths off until you reach a junction. Bear right, then immediately left towards a building with a white fascia (Patterson Ford Dealer), to pass a vehicle barrier and join the disused railway line you left earlier. **D**

Turn left and walk along the cycle path under two adjacent bridges before proceeding through a sheltered cutting. At the point where the pylons carrying the overhead electricity cables bear off to the left and houses appear on the right, leave the path and go right on the narrow path for about 50 yards to the end of a cul-de-sac. **E**

Turn right and walk down the road from the cul-de-sac passing, on your left, the relatively modern Parish Church of St Mark (1967). At the T-junction, with The Beaumont pub to your right, turn left and continue for a few hundred yards to Shiremoor Metro Station and the end of the walk.

ROUTE – A circular walk through fields, along farm tracks and through a pleasant wooded dene

TERRAIN – On the level on footpaths and farm tracks with one short steep ascent

REFRESHMENTS – Pub near beginning of the walk

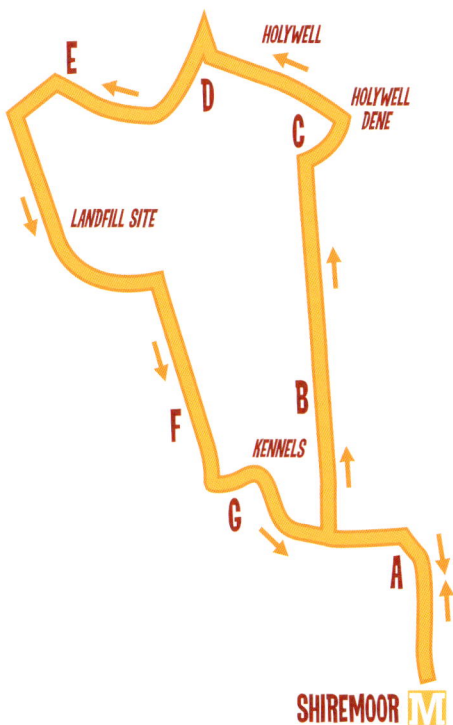

HOLYWELL

E

D

HOLYWELL DENE

C

LANDFILL SITE

B

F

KENNELS

G

A

SHIREMOOR M

Leave Shiremoor Metro Station and turn left at the road. Walk down the pavement to a T-junction, the Grey Horse pub is on the right-hand side. Cross the main road at the pedestrian lights a few yards along on your left. Turn right and walk a few yards to take the public footpath signposted for Earsdon and East Holywell, on the left just before the 50 mile speed limit sign. The narrow path, alongside the Earsdon View housing development, leads onto a wider track. Continue straight ahead with a hedgerow on your right and keep left at a junction as the tower of St Alban's Church at Earsdon becomes visible on your right. The track leads past an odd-looking building now incorporated into stables and a farm before reaching a metalled road. **A**

Turn left and walk along the side of the road for about 100 yards, passing the entrance to Church Farm, take a public footpath on your left via a vehicle barrier. Take the right-hand fork broad track with a hedge on your left and fields on your right. At a junction of tracks, take care to follow the second public bridleway ahead to the right. You immediately pass two utility poles on your right. Continue ahead until you arrive at a road opposite stables at Old School House, East Holywell. **B**

Cross the road, turn right and after a few yards, turn left to follow the public footpath sign "Holywell Grange Farm 1/3 m Holywell 1m". Walk along the broad farm track and pass the farmhouse on your right. Continue ahead for several hundred yards and at a fork continue straight ahead on the narrow path with a hedgerow on your left and extensive fields on your right. At a junction of paths, continue straight ahead on the narrow path, with the hedgerow on your left, and follow the path into the woods of Holywell Dene. **C**

Continue ahead as the path broadens out and makes its way round to the right to cross a footbridge over the Seaton Burn. Use the left fork to climb the short distance up the steep bankside to some houses. Turn left and follow the metalled path round the perimeter of the estate, keeping the woods on your left. Ignore paths off and as the line of trees come to an end, the path terminates at a rear road at the end of Newburgh Avenue. **D**

Walk a couple of paces up the bankside to the iron railings. Turn left and after a few yards bear left as the railings go off towards the right. Walk along the edge of the field with a hedgerow on your left until you reach the corner of the woods ahead and the houses are visible across to your left. Turn right to descend the narrow path between the hawthorn bushes. Cross the stone footbridge and continue, with fields on your left and the burn below on your right, until eventually you leave the path to exit at a road via a kissing gate. To your left is the entrance to the Civic Amenity depot and the landfill site. **E**

Cross over the road to take the path almost opposite which goes between a hedgerow and a wire fence. Beyond the fence you may catch a glimpse of a pond. Go through the kissing gate at the T-junction, with more stables ahead, and turn left. Follow the narrow green path as it crosses a footbridge and then climbs to come parallel with a railway. Proceed ahead with the railway on your right and trees on your left. The trees mask the landfill site for most of the way until the hedgerow ends and a perimeter fence appears. Continue on the track as it bears left behind the site with the perimeter fence on your left for about 400 yards. Then carry on as the path narrows between fields. When the path meets a broader track, turn right and continue to the end of the track to meet a road. **F**

Turn right and follow the road for about 400 yards, passing the motor dealers premises, to arrive at a right-hand bend a short distance before the entrance to Backworth Village. Cross the road with care and go down the metalled road on the opposite side for a few yards and bear left to enter the grounds of Holywest Kennels (you should hear the dogs even if you don't see the sign!). **G**

Although your route may appear rather unlikely at first, just continue straight ahead. The right of way leads between the kennels and the private bungalow on your right and you soon pass a red brick building on your right before joining a reassuring green track with fences on either side. As the path bears right, you will see a marshy area on your left which attracts bird-life. The path climbs a short way and becomes uneven in places. Proceed ahead with an old hedgerow on your right until you meet a surfaced track.

Turn left and walk for about 100 yards to the junction of paths that you met on the outward journey. Continue ahead with the fence on your left and the hedgerow on your right. Here you will get a good view of St Alban's Church at Earsdon, as you retrace your steps back to the road and Church Farm. Turn right and walk along the road for about 100 yards to take the public footpath on the right, signposted "Grey Horse ⅓". **A**

Follow the track for a few hundred yards and then retrace your steps along the path between the fields to the main road. Cross at the pedestrian lights and walk ahead with the Grey Horse on your left back to Shiremoor Metro Station and the end of the walk.

Shiremoor to West Monkseaton
(3.5 miles)

ROUTE – Across country to Earsdon then through fields to West Monkseaton

TERRAIN – Mainly on the level and mostly using field paths which can be muddy

REFRESHMENTS – A pub near the start, two pubs in Earsdon and a pub near the end of the walk

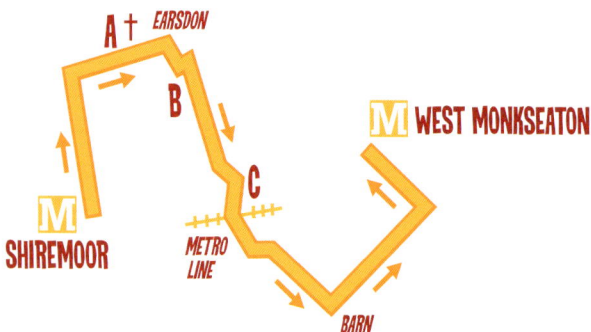

Leave Shiremoor Metro Station and turn left at the road. Walk down the pavement to a T-junction, the Grey Horse pub is on the right-hand side. Cross the main road at the pedestrian lights a few yards along on your left. Turn right and walk a few yards to take the public footpath signposted for Earsdon and East Holywell, on the left just before the 50 mile speed limit sign. The narrow path, alongside the Earsdon View housing development, leads onto a wider track. Continue straight ahead with a hedgerow on your right and keep left at a junction as the tower of St Alban's Church at Earsdon becomes visible on your right. The track leads past an odd-looking building now incorporated into stables and a farm before reaching a road. Cross the road with care and turn right to follow the pavement to Earsdon. You reach the entrance to the grounds of St Alban's Church (1837), where an information panel provides some details about the church and the memorial to a tragic mining accident in 1862. **A**

(An important feature in the graveyard is the Hartley Disaster Memorial. If you wish to visit this go behind the church tower, walk a few yards, go down the stepped path and continue a short distance to the memorial).

From the churchyard entrance, carry on in the same direction as before passing The Cannon Inn on your right. Proceed ahead through this pleasant village with its blend of Victorian and later properties. You pass Earsdon Methodist Church (1886) on your left and the War Memorial on your right and come to a T-junction with the Red Lion pub on your right. Turn right to cross the road with care at the traffic island. Follow the pavement as it bears right, with the pub on your right. Cross the main road using the pedestrian traffic lights. Turn left and walk a few yards then turn right and go through the gap in the fence to join a field path. **B**

Proceed ahead, with a hedgerow on your left. At the field boundary go into the next field. Turn right and follow the line of the hedgerow, now on your right. After about 50 yards turn left to follow the field boundary with the fence/hedgerow on your right. Carry on passing a playing field on your left, until you reach a public footpath sign (which confirms that you have come from Earsdon). Walk ahead, with the hedgerow now on your left, to come to another public footpath sign. Don't go into the housing estate ahead but turn right. Walk ahead, following the line of the hedgerow on your left as it bears left. At the field corner, go through the gap and cross the style. Turn right and proceed to the public footpath sign, next to the Metro line, ahead. **C**

Go through the gate and, with extreme care, cross the Metro line and walk straight ahead. At the field boundary turn left and after 50 yards turn right. Walk ahead with the hedgerow on your right towards some farm buildings in the distance. Where a broad firm track comes in from the right, carry straight on to a crossing of paths, just before a barn. Turn left and walk to the houses ahead. Carry on along Cauldwell Avenue to a main road (A192). Turn left, then cross to the other side at the traffic lights. Turn left and walk ahead, passing The Hunting Lodge pub on the left, to arrive at West Monkseaton Metro Station and the end of the walk.

↗ **ROUTE** – An initial walk through a residential area then across country to Holywell Dene. Follows the line of the dene to Seaton Sluice and returns via the coastal path to Monkseaton

🎿 **TERRAIN** – Mainly on the level with one or two gentle inclines. Most of the route is on metalled paths, pavements and surfaced tracks

☕ **REFRESHMENTS** – Two pubs and a tea room in Seaton Sluice and a pub in Whitley Lodge towards the end of the walk

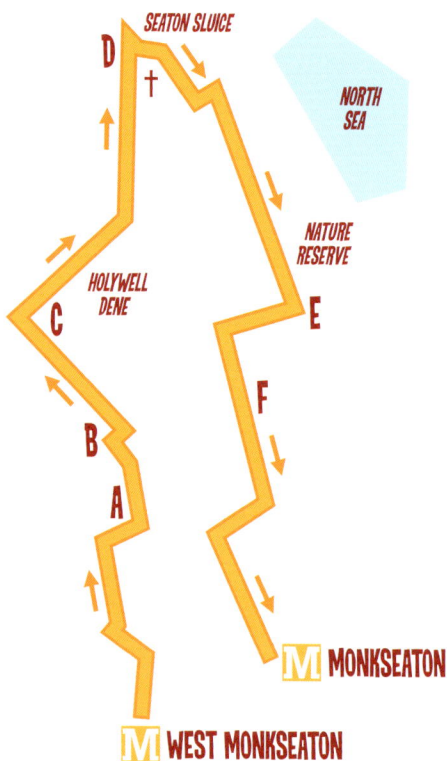

Exit West Monkseaton Metro Station and turn right. After a few yards, just after a bus stop, turn right and go down the ramp to reach Sunningdale. Cross the road and carry on in the same direction on the metalled path. When the path meets a road, opposite a sign for St Andrews Close, turn left and after a few yards turn left again and proceed to a T-junction. Turn right, walk a few yards then cross the road to walk along Meadow-field. At the end of the road continue ahead on the metalled path. At the end of the path, bear right and go, via three metal posts, onto another path and walk ahead past a sculpture of sheep. Do not go beyond the little metal barrier in front of you but bear left. Follow the path and shortly bear right to join a road near a bus shelter. Cross the road with care and turn right to walk along the pavement, with the trees on your left. At the roundabout cross the road with care to enter Red House Drive. **A**

Walk ahead, initially past an interesting variety of houses on both sides then past open country on the left. Eventually you come to Haddington Road on your right, at which point Red House Drive becomes Beaumont Drive. Carry on and, just past Beaconsfield Close on your right, take the public footpath on the left. Follow the narrow surfaced path to exit onto a broad surfaced track. **B**

Turn left and walk along the track which follows the line of a disused railway. You pass a farm on the right. The small round building with a conical roof is a gingan, once a common feature of farms in the North-East, incorporating a horse-driven mechanism for threshing grain. After going under a bridge carry straight on. Eventually the path descends between trees and you come to a second bridge. On the right there is an information panel with details about Holywell Dene. Take the path on the left immediately before the bridge and follow this to meet another path. Turn right and walk ahead over the bridge. **C**

Keep on the path as it runs above the attractive Holywell Dene on your right. Over to your left in the distance is an obelisk. To the left of this, you can see Seaton Delaval Hall, designed by Sir John Vanburgh for Admiral George Delaval (both of whom died before its completion in 1729). At a point where the path narrows, ignore a narrow path off to the right and proceed ahead. You pass below a farmhouse on your left and the path descends into woodland. At a T-junction of paths, bear left. A short distance further on, bear right to go through the little wooden barrier and follow the narrow path as it gradually descends towards the Seaton Burn. Follow the path and come to a bridge; there is another Holywell Dene information panel here. Go over the stile, turn right and walk across the bridge, then go over the stile on the left and walk ahead. Carry on, past a path to the right (which leads to a small pond with an observation platform), and, after a short ascent, you come to a T-junction of paths. Turn left and continue in the same direction. Follow this pleasant path, passing through woodland and attractive riverside scenery, until you come to another information panel. Carry on, and where the path turns right, continue over the grass until you reach an information panel which gives historical and other details about Seaton Sluice. **D**

Exit onto the pavement. To your right is St Paul's Church (converted from a former community hall in 1961). Cross the road with care, and go into Collywell Bay Road. There are plenty of refreshment possibilities here. On the left is The Kings Arms; on your right The Waterford Arms, famous for its fish and chips. A few yards further on, just past the War Memorial on the left, is the Castaways Tea Shop. To continue the walk, proceed ahead along Collywell Bay Road. Opposite number 48, go onto the footpath and follow the direction of the fingerpost to "Coastline and Countryside". Keep to the path as it follows the line of the bay. In the distance over to your left you might see the offshore wind farm at Blyth. The path bears right and continues along the cliff tops. Eventually you emerge into a small car park. Go straight ahead and follow the coastal path. St Mary's Island lighthouse is ahead on your left. Continue on the broad path, ignoring paths off to the left. (If you wish to visit the island bear left, opposite a pedestrian/cycleway sign, and follow the path which has two benches). On your left you pass a succession of information panels with viewpoints overlooking St Mary's Island Local Nature Reserve, a haven for sea birds and plant life. The path exits to the right of a car park. **E**

Turn right and follow the road to its junction with a busy main road. Bear right, walk ahead and, at convenient point, cross to the other side. Continue ahead, passing a cemetery on your left, to arrive at two public footpath signs near a sharp right-hand bend. Turn left and follow the narrow path, passing the cemetery on your left and the golf course on your right. The path passes the gardens of houses on your left and eventually exits onto a pavement. **F**

Turn right and walk ahead. On the right you pass the entrance to Whitley Bay Golf Club and, later, the Kittiwake pub. When you reach a roundabout, cross the road with care and turn right to walk up the road (Monkseaton Drive). After passing the last house on the left and then a bus stop, bear left along the metalled path. Proceed ahead on the pleasant tree-lined path, passing playing fields on your left and then walking behind houses on your left and the Metro line on the right. Exit onto a pavement and bear right to walk a few yards to a busy road (Marine Drive). Cross the road with care. (At busy times, you can use the pedestrian crossing further along on the right). Proceed to Monkseaton Metro Station and the end of the walk.

Seaton Sluice Harbour

➤ **ROUTE** - Along a cycleway and field paths to St Mary's Island and then by the sea front to Whitley Bay.

🏃 **TERRAIN** - On (sometimes muddy) field paths and metalled paths and pavements. There are some stiles to cross

☕ **REFRESHMENTS** - On St Mary's Island, along the sea front and in Whitley Bay

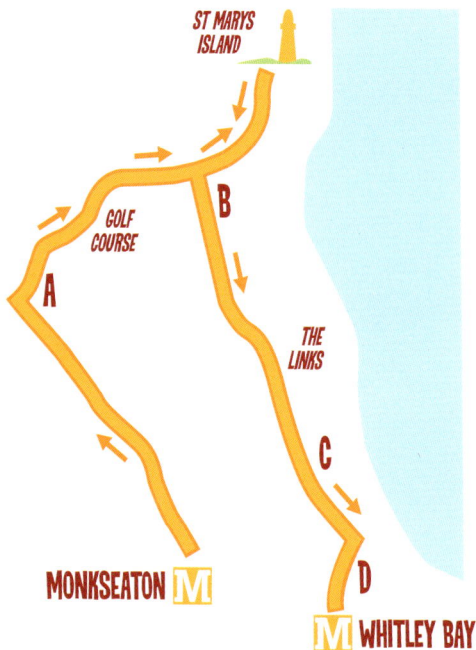

ST MARYS
ISLAND

GOLF
COURSE

A

B

THE
LINKS

C

D

MONKSEATON Ⓜ

Ⓜ WHITLEY BAY

Leave Monkseaton Metro Station: from Platform 1, through the covered ramp onto a busy road (Marine Avenue); from Platform 2 , turn left and walk to Marine Avenue. Cross the road with care to Hartley Avenue. (At busy times, you can use the pedestrian crossing further along on the left). Walk to the end of Hartley Avenue and follow the path round the back of the changing rooms of the Churchill Playing Fields. Then bear right along the metalled cycle track. Keep on the track which goes through a subway (which may be flooded after heavy rain) and runs between houses before emerging into an open area near a golf course. After a few hundred yards, at a crossing of paths (before the path reaches the farm buildings ahead on the right) look out for a stile on your right. **A**

Go over the stile. There is a Whitley Bay Golf Club notice almost immediately on your right. Walk to the end of the path and cross the stile on your left. Bear right and follow the field boundary with the hedge on your right to a public footpath sign at the field corner. Cross the stile and go straight ahead along the field boundary, with the fence on your left. At the end of the field, cross the stile. Turn left and proceed along the path, which runs between the golf links and farm fields. At a crossing of paths, turn right between the walls of a former railway bridge. Soon you emerge at a corner of a busy road. Walk ahead on the pavement towards the sea. At a convenient point, cross the road and walk to the junction of the main road and the road leading to St Mary's Island. **B**

To go to the island, follow the road to the causeway. Check the tide tables there to see if it safe to cross. If it is, go across the causeway to the island. The comforting blink of the lighthouse's warning beacon served as a navigational aid from 1898 to 1984. If you're in the right season (and the right state of fitness!) you can climb to the top, from where you can enjoy magnificent views. After your trip, retrace your steps across the causeway and back to point. **B**

Proceed along the pavement towards Whitley Bay, where a white, domed building, all that remains of the former fairground, called the Spanish City, is the most prominent landmark. The open area on your left is called "The Links" and is used as a miniature golf course in the summer months. As you approach The Briardene pub, on the other side of the road, just before the 30 mile sign turn left onto a metalled path which descends to the lower promenade. Continue in the same direction. You pass The Rendevous Café and then a fountain erected in May 1937 on the occasion of the coronation of George VI and Queen Elizabeth. Shortly, you pass the changing rooms of the Panama Swimming Club (whose members brave the cold North Sea for their annual New Year's Day swim!). Carry on to a junction of paths with steps ahead on the right. (To avoid the steps you can turn right and make your way along paths to the War Memorial). Go up the steps and proceed to the War Memorial, commemorating the fallen from both World Wars. **C**

Walk ahead and up the slope to join the pavement and pass some sculptured metal seats and a Waterside Trail information panel. Proceed ahead with the sea on your left. Continue until the road divides at the Rex Hotel. **D**

Take the right-hand fork past the hotel on your left and proceed ahead. You are now on South Parade (confirmed by a sign a little further on). Carry on, past the trendy pubs, until you reach a busy crossroads in the town centre. Turn left, as indicated by the sign for the Metro Station, and walk along Victoria Terrace to Whitley Bay Metro Station and the end of the walk.

St Mary's Lighthouse

➜ **ROUTE** – Through interesting parts of Whitley Bay and along the sea front to Cullercoats and Tynemouth

🚶 **TERRAIN** – Mainly along pavements and promenades. There is a short walk around a small lake (which can be omitted)

☕ **REFRESHMENTS** – Wide range of possibilities throughout the walk

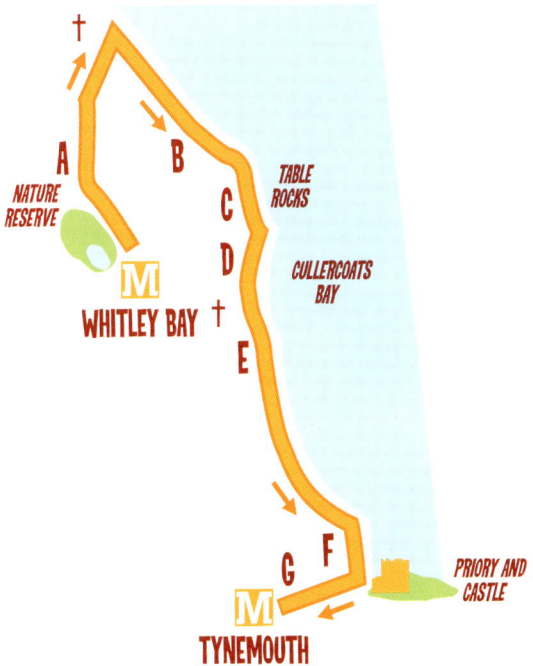

Exit from Whitley Bay Metro Station from Platform 1. (Platform 1 can be accessed from Platform 2 by either steps or ramps). Walk along the pathway and then straight ahead along Etal Avenue for about 200 yards. Turn left and walk along Holystone Avenue to the end. Turn right and walk the short distance to the junction of Burnside Road and a main road (Marden Road). On your right is The Quarry pub, which has a plaque outlining its history. Cross the busy road with care to reach the (unmarked) entrance to Marden Quarry Nature

Reserve, to the right of a large detached white house. A few yards beyond the entrance go into the car park on the right, where a notice board gives details of the former quarry and its transformation into a nature reserve by North Tyneside Council. Leave the car park and turn right onto the path which takes you a pleasant, short walk around the lake. **A**

After completing the circuit of the lake, exit the reserve and cross the road to The Quarry, then turn left and proceed along the pavement towards the roundabout ahead. Follow the pavement as it curves to the right over the Metro line. Carry on, past shops and offices, into the centre of town at a busy junction. St Paul's Church (1864) with its unusual truncated spire is on the left. Turn right and walk to the traffic lights. Cross the road and proceed along Park Avenue. Continue down, passing the red-stone Whitley Bay Baptist Church, until the road divides. Take the right-hand road (still Park Avenue) and carry on to the promenade. Turn right and proceed ahead to the Rex Hotel. **B**

Continue along the sea front on the pavement or, opposite Victoria Avenue, you can descend to the lower promenade to walk in the same direction. If you walk on the lower level, when you reach a tiled roof brick shelter, look below to Table Rocks. Here, there is a natural pool, formerly used as the "table rocks swimming pool" but now too dangerous for such activities. Rejoin the pavement and carry on to where the road bends to the right. **C**

Bear left along the wide pavement in front of the houses at Southcliff. At the end, turn right. Walk a few yards and then turn right and go to the end of the road (Norma Crescent). Turn left and follow the pavement along the main road. Go past the little boat yard and The Queens Head to arrive at Cullercoats Bay, a favourite place for painters and photographers over the years. The Cullercoats lifeboat station is situated here. It is also the location for the University of Newcastle Dove Marine Laboratory, an important centre for the study of the local marine environment. **D**

Proceed ahead. You soon arrive at an information board which gives historical details about Cullercoats, as well as indicating nearby points of interest. Continue in the same direction. Ahead, in the distance, are Tynemouth's North Pier and the ruins of Tynemouth Priory and Castle. As you leave Cullercoats, you pass the impressive St George's Church

(1884), whose tower and spire are 180 feet high. The First World War memorial is outside the east end. **E**

Below you are the Long Sands. There are a number of access points if you prefer to walk along the beach. Carrying on along the pavement, you pass, on your right, the Blue Reef Aquarium, and The Park Hotel. In a short while you pass, on your left, a mini-golf course. Over the road is Tynemouth Park with its boating lake and The Clocktower Café. Continue in the same direction towards the end of the Long Sands. Near the end there is a Waterside Trail notice board which gives historical and environmental information about the area. Below, there is a rock pool, converted from the former open air swimming pool in 1996. Carry on, as the pavement follows the curve of King Edward's Bay with its Short Sands. Over the road is the splendid sweep of the houses in Percy Gardens. Shortly you pass the Gibraltar Rock pub and, then, the imposing bulk of Tynemouth Priory and Castle, now managed by English Heritage. Three kings were buried here and this is reflected in the three crowns in the crest of North Tyneside Council. In a few yards you arrive at a clock tower and Tynemouth village. **F**

Turn right and make your way along Front Street with its fascinating collection of shops, pubs and cafes. If you want to see an intriguing example of the taxidermist's art, you can pop into the Turks Head Hotel (A plaque outside explains the significance). At the end of Front Street, on the right-hand side, you can turn right, where there are more shops and cafes. At the end of Front Street, on the left-hand side, is the Land of Green Ginger, a shopping mall, full of nooks and crannies, occupying a former church. **G**

To complete the walk, cross the road and go through the little park which runs alongside the 19th-century Huntington Place. In the park there is a statue of Queen Victoria (1902) and two war memorials. You can follow the road on your left to arrive at Tynemouth Metro Station. Or follow the alternative directions to the right, which avoids steps, to reach Platform 1 for train departures to Newcastle via South Gosforth. An information board in the station gives details of Saturday and Sunday markets held here.

ROUTE - Through Tynemouth village and along the River Tyne to North Shields

TERRAIN - Mainly on the level on pavements and metalled paths. Towards the end there is a steep ascent via steps. The steps, but not the steep ascent, can be avoided by taking the alternative route as indicated

REFRESHMENTS - A wide variety of places in Tynemouth and North Shields

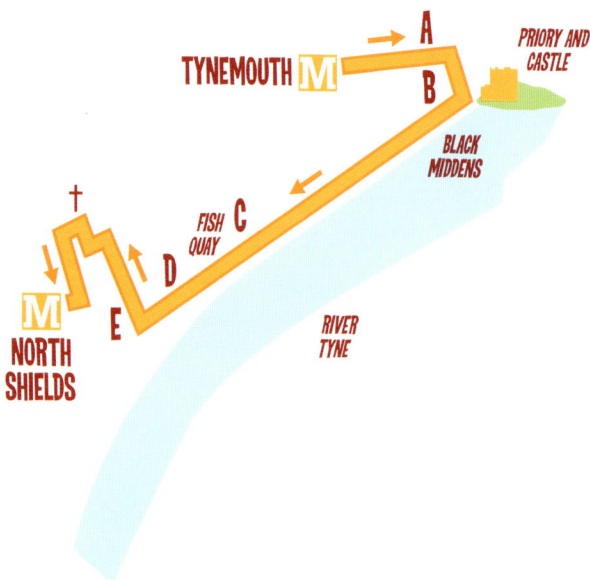

Leave Tynemouth Station from Platform 2. (Platform 2 can be accessed from Platform 1 either by steps and a bridge, or, exit the station and follow the sign "Access via road bridge"). Near the exit there are some notice boards with interesting information, including details of markets which are held on the station concourse on Saturdays and Sundays. Emerge opposite Kings School. Turn left and follow the road as it bears right past a pleasant terrace. There is a plaque on Number 9 explaining Garibaldi's stay there in 1854. The small park on your left has two war memorials and the Queen Victoria Monument (1902) by Alfred Gilbert. Cross at the traffic lights and walk ahead, passing the Land of Green Ginger shopping mall on your right. Carry on along Front Street to the clock tower at the end. **A**

Turn right and proceed down the road to Tynemouth Haven. On your left are the ruins of Tynemouth Priory and Castle. Over to your right is the Collingwood Monument (1845) designed by John Dobson (1787-1865) the famous architect who was born in North Shields. The tall statue is by John Lough (1798-1876), the highly-regarded Northumbrian sculptor. The monument was paid for by a grateful public, proud of one of the heroes of Trafalgar. Now, follow the path by the side of the road as it ascends to the Spanish Battery. You might like to go left onto the headland to enjoy the views, or to the right to visit the Watch House and Museum. To continue the walk you need to carry on in the same direction and follow the path which soon descends towards the river. On reaching the riverside you will see a plaque referring to the notorious Black Middens. **B**

Proceed along the riverside path with the river on your left. Above on the right is the Collingwood Monument. You come to an information panel near the Black Middens. The two large white towers ahead are the Low Light and the High Light, former navigational aids for vessels sailing into the Tyne. Carry on, eventually passing a small sandy beach and a car park. When you reach a road, cross over and follow the sign "Pedestrian Ferry ½". Walk to the New Dolphin pub and bear left to the front of the pub with a modern sculpture and a whale jawbone outside. **C**

Walk ahead, passing the Fish Quay on your left. On the right is a miscellany of fishmongers, pubs and cafes. Wm Wight Ltd's shop usually displays some amusing messages. Just before the tall blue corrugated metal building (the ice house), on the right you arrive at Ropery Stairs. **D**

You now have a choice of routes. To avoid the steep steps, continue straight ahead to a junction near The Porthole pub, turn right and walk up the steep hill. At the T-junction, turn right and proceed to North Shields Metro Station. Otherwise, turn right and go up Ropery Stairs. At the top, turn left and walk along Tyne Street. Looking back you get a good view of the High and Low Lights. At the end of the street you come to a Waterside Trail information panel and, nearby, an anchor, serving as a memorial "For all those lost at sea". A plaque on the Registry Office building outlines its history. **E**

Turn right and walk along Howard Street, taking care crossing other roads. You come to Northumberland Square. Go into the little park, bear left at the Wooden Dolly sculpture of a Cullercoats fishwife. Follow the path diagonally through the park to the crossroads. Turn right, cross the road and proceed along Upper Camden Street. At the T-junction turn left. Over the road is Christ Church (1668), built as the parish church of Tynemouth. Walk ahead and turn left. Proceed along Church Way, cross at the crossroads with care and walk to the loading bay area. Turn right. Walk ahead and go down the narrow alley. Walk to the clock tower on your left and turn right to arrive at North Shields Metro Station and the end of the walk.

New Dolphin Pub

ROUTE - Through North Shields to the River Tyne and across by the pedestrian ferry. The ferry departs every 30 minutes on the hour and half-hour. Through South Shields via a Roman fort and the attractive North Marine Park

TERRAIN - There is an initial steep descent. In South Shields, after a steady climb from the river, the walk is mostly on the level on pavements and metalled paths

REFRESHMENTS - Several pubs and cafes in the town centres and along the route

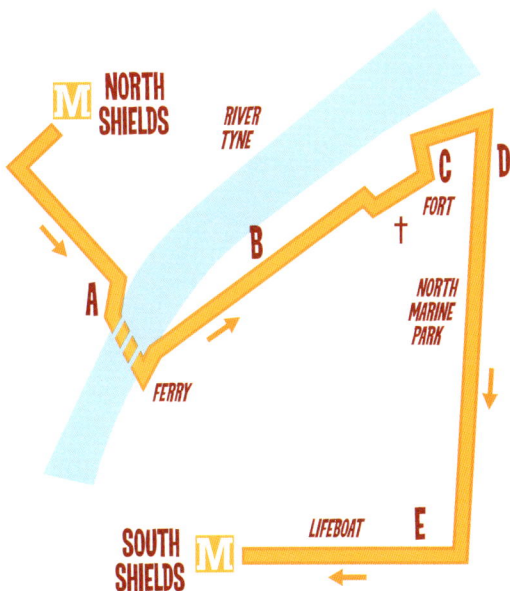

Leave North Shields Metro Station and turn right. In a few yards, turn right to follow the sign "Pedestrian Ferry". Proceed ahead and turn left into Borough Road. Follow the road as it descends towards the river. At the bottom of the hill, turn right and walk a short distance, then turn left into Ferry Mews. Board the ferry. **A**

Enjoy the crossing! After disembarking, go to the end of the walkway and turn left. Walk for 25 yards and then turn right and walk to the Alum Ale House pub on your left. Turn left at the T-junction and proceed ahead. At the roundabout bear right and follow the road, climbing quite steeply, as it bears left and crosses a railway bridge. Immediately below the bridge on the left, is, literally, the end of the line. You can also enjoy some extensive views of the river. On the riverside promenade you can see the *Spirit of South Shields* sculpture by Irene Brown. Just beyond the bridge, turn left onto the metalled path. **B**

Follow the path past the statue of Dolly Peel (1782-1857) whose fascinating story is told on the accompanying information panel. Continue on the path. Below on the left there are several little boatyards on the riverside. The path rejoins the main pavement. From here, looking over the river to North Shields, the two tall white buildings in the foreground are the High Light and Low Light, which for many years served as navigational aids. Cross the road and proceed along Mile End Road. After a few yards turn left and follow the path past the beautifully maintained war memorial and graveyard. Unusually, the memorial honours the men from just one North Shields street, who fought and died in the First World War. The church over to the right is St Stephen and St Aidan (1846). At a junction of paths turn left, walk about 50 yards and at the railings turn right. Walk ahead and go up three steps. Turn left and follow the road round to the right with the railings on your left. Just after Hadrian Nursery School, turn left and follow the railings towards the church. Continue ahead to the junction at the People's Mission. Turn left past the People's Mission and walk to Arbeia Roman Fort and Museum on the right. **C**

After visiting Arbeia, leave the grounds, turn right and walk towards the river. At the T-junction turn right and proceed along Greens Place. You pass Wellesley Court, formerly the River Tyne Pilot Offices, and The Beacon pub. Walk ahead to the Lawe Beacons (1832), a plaque outlines its significance. Ignore the gateposts on your left as you bear right for 30 yards before turning left into the park. **D**

Follow the pink line which takes you left at a crossing of paths. You come to a small plaque at The Lawe Top. From the top of the nearby steps there are splendid sea views. On the beach below you can see the bronze figures of the *Conversation Piece* sculpture by Juan Muñoz. Keep following the pink line until you reach a crossing of paths with a lamp post in the centre. Go straight ahead, now following the yellow line, passing a second lamp post before reaching the Westovian Theatre. Turn right and walk the short distance to the lifeboat memorial and the clock tower (1887). **E**

Walk ahead to the crossroads. Cross over and continue in the same direction along the road (Ocean Road) with its fascinating collection of ethnic restaurants and takeaways. The road becomes pedestrianised as you come to the town centre. You pass the Museum and Art Gallery and a statue in memory of John Simpson Kirkpatrick, a hero of the First World War. Carry straight on to the South Shields Metro Station and the end of the walk.

The Shields Ferry

ROUTE – From the new housing development of Northumberland Park, through Backworth Village to the outskirts of Killingworth to Palmersville in a largely rural setting

TERRAIN – Level-walking mainly along old waggonways, a very short section on a road, otherwise on metalled paths

REFRESHMENTS – A pub near the beginning and end of the walk

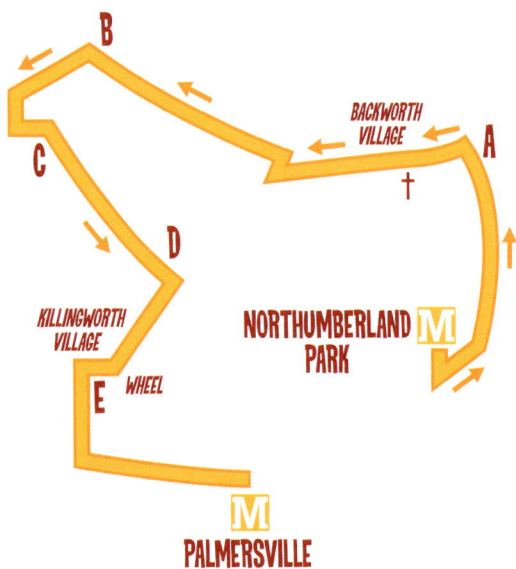

Turn right at the exit from Northumberland Park Metro Station and walk a short distance past the car park to a main road. Turn left and proceed ahead for about a quarter of a mile until you are almost opposite The Blue Bell pub. Turn left at the blue Cycleway 10 sign to follow a track which leads over the Metro line and eventually bears right. You pass a works entrance on your left. Ahead on the horizon you may see St Alban's Church at Earsdon. At a T-junction turn left in the direction of the Cycleway 10 sign and follow the metalled path. Carry on, ignoring a public footpath off to the right. The path narrows and there are hedgerows on either side. You may hear dogs barking as you pass a metal barrier, then an old boat on your right and stables on your left to exit onto a road at the entrance to Holywest Kennels. **A**

Turn left and with care cross to the right-hand side of the road to continue ahead for a short distance, past the Backworth Village sign and over the level-crossing. The walk now continues on the pavement and you pass an interesting variety of properties. Opposite St John the Baptist Church (1886), follow the road as it bears right. At a convenient spot, cross over to the other side of the road to continue ahead with the War Memorial on your left. On the right there are some attractive cottages originally built in the 19th century for the Duke of Northumberland's estate workers. At the end of the village, the path leads to an open area. Follow the path, passing a telephone box on your left. Leave the path as it turns to the left, just before a road and turn right to walk a short distance, on the grass verge to a T-junction. Turn left to proceed on the pavement alongside the B1322. In about ½ mile you arrive at a junction with a road bridge on your left. Cross the road with great care and continue in the same direction (Seghill) as before, for a further 150 yards, to the third of three Cycleway 10 signs just before a parking area. **B**

Turn left to follow a track that leads under a road bridge. Continue ahead on the tree-lined track past a wooden barrier after which the view over the adjacent fields becomes a little more open. Eventually you arrive at a crossing of tracks at a sign "Waggonway". Turn left and walk along the field boundary with the wire fence on your right. At a fork in the track take the path to the right which after a short distance turns to the left and leads to a main road and a roundabout. Bear left and follow the pavement to the pedestrian lights. Cross over the road and turn left. Continue ahead for about 150 yards to the slip road leading to "Farm Shop" (Hillheads). **C**

Bear right to follow the slip road, ignoring the bridle path to Killingworth on the right, and walk ahead with the wooden railings on your left. When you arrive at a metal sign "Waggonways", bear right and follow the broad track, ignoring any paths off, until you exit at a road. **D**

Turn right and follow the road as it passes East House Farm and skirts the residential area of Killingworth. Eventually, after the 30 mile speed limit sign, the path bends to the right. After about a further 100 yards, on the left-hand side of the road, there is a sign for Killingworth Village, and just beyond it another "Waggonways" sign. E

Cross the road with care to pick up this track as you pass a huge metal wheel in commemoration of the bicentenary of the birth of the locally-born steam locomotive inventor George Stephenson. Follow the track until you reach a road. Turn left, cross the road at a convenient place and walk ahead for about ½ mile past the Musketeer pub to Palmersville Metro Station and the end of the walk.

Killingworth – Stephenson's Wheel

Palmersville to Benton
(3.5 miles)

↱ ROUTE - Takes you through a nature reserve with a pond frequented by bird life and a country park with splendid panoramic views of North Tyneside and beyond

🚶 TERRAIN - Mainly on surfaced tracks but with some sections on rougher footpaths that can be muddy. Involves a steady climb with a quite steep descent

☕ REFRESHMENTS - Pub just beyond Palmersville Metro Station and facilities in the Rising Sun Country Park

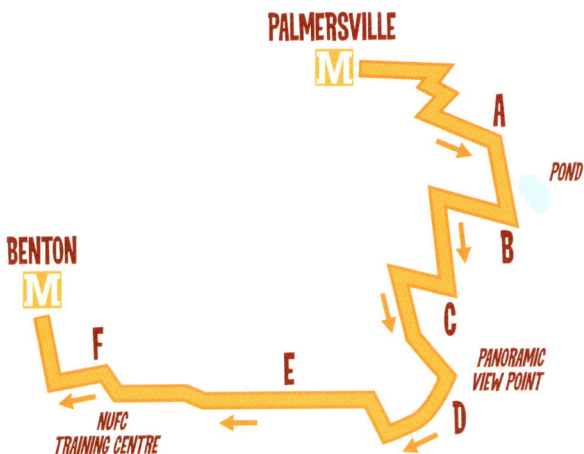

Exit from Palmersville Metro Station and turn right to follow the pavement to The Wheatsheaf. Immediately after the pub, turn right and continue for about 200 yards until you see the sign on the opposite side of the road for the Rising Sun Country Park. Cross the road with care (at busy times you can use the pedestrian crossing 200 yards ahead) and proceed down the metalled road leading towards the country park. You soon leave the surrounds of the retail complex and are walking between hedgerows with meadowland on one side and a paddock on the other. After a few hundred yards, leave the road via a kissing gate at a public footpath sign on your right. A (To visit the Rising Sun Countryside Centre, refreshments available, you need to follow the road for a further 200 yards).

Follow the path as it descends gently towards a wooded area.

Pass beneath an interesting wooden sculpture and turn almost immediately left at a junction of paths. You pass a metal sculpture of a mole and are quickly into a pleasant glade, walking across duck boarding and passing benches where you can take a rest if needs must. You soon arrive at a stone hide through which you can view the nature reserve's pond and admire the bird life and wild flowers. Continue on the clear path and go through the kissing gate next to a metal gate onto a broad track. **B**

Turn right, walk for about 150 yards and turn left to leave the track opposite a metal gate. Fork almost immediately left to take the path towards the edge of the wood (ignoring the waymarked countryside trail to the right). Walk along the perimeter of the wood on what can sometimes be a rather muddy path. When the path bears right at the corner of the wood, after a few yards look out for a small wooden footbridge on your left. Cross over the footbridge and walk straight ahead with a fence on your left and an old hedgerow on your right to meet a metalled lane. **C**

Turn right and proceed along the lane for about 150 yards until you reach, on your left what appear to be two finger posts without their fingers! Turn sharp left through the wide wooden barrier and continue ahead in the same direction along a broad track which is stony in parts. The track climbs gradually to meet a junction of paths. Turn left to climb past a waymarked post and reach the top of the rise and a splendid panoramic viewpoint. Here you have an example of the effective reclamation of land, as you are now on the reclaimed spoil heap of a major coal mine, the Rising Sun Colliery, that closed in 1969. **D**

From here there are views of North Tyneside and beyond. To the south-west, far beyond the cranes of the shipyards you may even be able to see the Grecian-looking Penshaw Monument in County Durham, while to the north-west beyond North Tyneside College, you may be able to discern the Simonside Hills. To continue the walk, retrace your steps to the waymarked post. Bear left and descend on the broad track, soon passing a further waymarked post. Some 125 yards beyond this second post, bear right to leave the track at a short (unwaymarked) post and follow the grassy track as it rises slightly before dropping quite steeply for about 150 yards before bearing right between bushes to reach a metal gate just in front of some houses. Don't go through the gate, but instead turn right to follow the public bridleway, which can be muddy, as it proceeds past the houses on your left and trees on your right. At the end of the housing, with a public footpath sign on your right, turn left over a small footbridge. The track has housing on the left and fields on the right. You pass over two low vehicle hurdles as the track proceeds for a few hundred yards to arrive at a busy road at the entrance to Wallsend. **E**

Cross the road with care and follow the broad track as it continues ahead in the direction of the public footpath sign: "East Benton Farm 1/3 m 0.5Km; Whitley Road 2/3 m 1Km". The track leads past the farm buildings and then a row of cottages before crossing a bridge over a railway. Continue along the track until you meet a metalled lane at the entrance to the Newcastle United Training Centre. Turn right and proceed up the lane a short distance to reach the main road (Whitley Road). **F**

Turn left and follow the pavement as far as the traffic lights at Station Road. Cross over with care and proceed down Station Road for about 200 yards until you see the sign for the Metro station which is on the left-hand side. Cross over the road and make your way to Benton Metro Station and the end of the walk.

→ **ROUTE** - Takes you past the Newcastle United Training Centre and Academy, skirts around a modern housing development and goes along a tree-lined old waggonway

🚶 **TERRAIN** - Level walking along surfaced paths and firm tracks. There are ten shallow steps and a moderately steep climb at the end of the walk

☕ **REFRESHMENTS** - Pub about half-way; another pub and cafes near the end

---

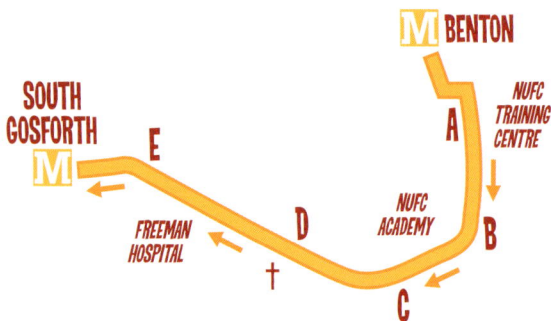

From Benton Metro Station, exit from Platform 1 directly onto Station Approach Road; from Platform 2, cross over the bridge to join the same road. Walk along the pavement for 100 yards or so to join the main road at The Beeches. Continue in the same direction to the traffic lights at the junction with Whitley Road. Cross over the busy Whitley Road with great care. Turn left and walk for about 250 yards, passing an entrance to Whitley Park sports ground to reach a metalled lane opposite a children's play area. Turn right and go down the lane the short distance to the entrance to the Newcastle United Training Centre. **A**

Bear right to go down a broad track and follow the track as it winds its way between the sports fields. Immediately on the left are the Newcastle United training facilities, while on the right is Whitley Park. You soon walk past some grazing land on your right, beyond which the white buildings are those of the Coach Lane Campus of Northumbria University. A short distance further along the track, on the right, are the Newcastle United Academy facilities for young players and you might be able to do some talent spotting! The track eventually draws close to the main London to Edinburgh railway line before meeting a metalled path beside a bridge over the railway. **B**

Don't cross the bridge, but instead turn right and follow the path behind modern housing on your left. At a junction of paths bear right and continue along the path as it bears left between the houses. Cross two minor roads with care and proceed as far as the main road (Coach Lane). **C**

Turn left and cross the road at the pedestrian traffic lights. Walk straight ahead down the "Coxlodge Waggonway". This pleasant tree lined track soon passes a school (Heaton Manor) on the right. Cross the busy Newton Road with care and continue along the signposted waggonway, just to the left of the Newton Park pub. **D**

The track passes, on your right, two important sources of employment, the Department of Work and Pensions and the Inland Revenue offices. On the left, it passes St Francis Church (1953), and then the Freeman Hospital, renowned for its pioneering heart surgery. Another school (St Mary's RC Comprehensive) stands on the right before the track eventually reaches the main Benton Road where there are ten shallow steps down to the pavement. **E**

Turn left and proceed straight ahead, using the pedestrian lights to cross Freeman Road and Haddricks Mill Road to arrive at the Brandling Villa pub. Turn right, then left to make your way up Station Road (South Gosforth Bank). The pavement climbs quite steeply past a parade of shops with cafes before reaching South Gosforth Metro Station and the end of the walk.

West Jesmond to Jesmond (5 miles)

ROUTE - Across four of Newcastle's moors and through some interesting parts of Gosforth and Jesmond

TERRAIN - On the level, mainly along metalled paths, with short sections over grassland

REFRESHMENTS - A wide selection of hotels and restaurants in Jesmond

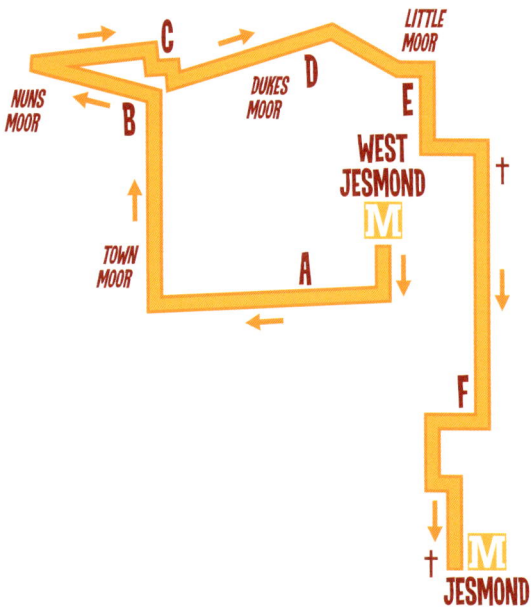

Leave West Jesmond Metro Station. From Platform 1, take the steps and subway or the ramp to cross to the other side of the line. Turn left. From Platform 2, turn left. Walk along Brentwood Avenue past shops and restaurants to a crossroads. Turn right and walk along the road (Forsyth Road). At a convenient spot, cross the road and carry on to the crossroads with a main road (Great North Road). Cross at the traffic lights to arrive at a blue gate. This is one of the entrances to the Town Moor, sometimes referred to as "Newcastle's lung". It is owned by the city for the benefit of Newcastle townsfolk who have free access but the grazing rights belong to the city's Freemen. **A**

Go onto the public footpath and walk ahead, via a gate, to a crossing of paths. The metal structure in the distance over to the left is St James' Park, the home of Newcastle United. Turn right and walk along the path with the tall lamp standards. Over to your right in the distance is the tall tower of St George's Church, Jesmond, which you pass later. Exit from the moor onto the pavement of a main road (Grandstand Road) at its junction with Kenton Road. Turn left and cross the road at the traffic lights. Bear right and walk a few yards to go through the gate on your left onto the Nuns Moor. **B**

Follow the line of the wall on your right. The grassy path runs roughly parallel to the wall, at distances varying between 20 and 100 yards from it. The Nuns Moor derives its name from the nuns of St Bartholomew's priory, a Benedictine order, who owned the land. Locally, it is usually referred to as the Cowgate Moor. You pass a tall block of flats and a terrace of modern three-storey properties. Just beyond the latter, leave the moor through a gate on your right onto a narrow alley running between garden fences. Exit the alley at its junction with Sheldon Grove and turn right. Proceed along the pavement. You need to cross the road at the green area in front of the flats (Montagu Court). Carry on in the same direction along the wide Montagu Avenue with its range of interesting properties. The width is accounted for because this was originally part of the carriageway leading to the home of the Montagu family at Denton. Walk to the junction with Kenton Road. Cross the road, using the traffic island to your left. Turn right and walk to the junction with Westfield. **C**

The building on the corner, now occupied by the car showroom, is on the site of the original grandstand (from which Grandstand Road got its name), erected in 1800 when there was a race track on the Town Moor. Walk along Westfield, past the art deco style Moor Court flats on the right. Immediately after Moor Court, turn right and walk along the alleyway to a public footpath sign. Turn left onto the Dukes Moor. Follow the narrow path which roughly parallels the garden walls over to your left. Carry on and exit the moor by a gate to a small grassed corner with seats. This was formerly known as "tittybottle corner" because Gosforth nursemaids used to congregate here for a chat while giving the babies their bottles. **D**

Cross High Street at the pedestrian lights and walk ahead. After a few yards cross Moor Road South and then turn right to cross the road to the public footpath sign opposite. Walk onto the Little Moor and follow the metalled path. Continue, past the allotments, to exit onto a main road. Turn right to walk a few yards and cross the road at the pedestrian lights. Turn left and walk to the junction at the traffic lights. **E**

Turn right and proceed along the road (Osborne Road). Carry on as the road bears to the left. At the junction, with the ornate white gateposts opposite, follow the road as it bears right then left and walk past St George's Church (1888). Its Italianate tower is a notable landmark hereabouts. Pass Acorn Road, which has interesting shops and a cafe. Shortly, you go through one of Newcastle's "in" places with numerous hotels and restaurants. Continue ahead and, just past Haldane Court flats, opposite a small parade of shops, turn into the road on the right (Haldane Terrace). **F**

Walk ahead to the T-junction. The Newcastle upon Tyne Church High School is opposite. Turn left and proceed to another T-junction, Jesmond United Reformed Church (1888) is on the opposite corner. Turn left and walk to the crossroads, then turn right and walk to the end of the road (Burdon Terrace). This is the last point for a refreshment stop. Willi's Coffee Shop is over the road and there are two pubs (The Collingwood Arms and The Bar at the Brandling) tucked away along the lane to the left of the coffee shop. To complete the walk, cross the road into Eskdale Terrace. Proceed ahead passing Central Newcastle High School and the Royal Grammar School to arrive at Jesmond Parish Church (1861) designed by John Dobson (1787-1865), the famous Newcastle architect. It was built in memory of the Revd Richard Clayton (1802-1856), a noted Christian leader on Tyneside in the 19th century. Turn left to walk to Jesmond Metro Station and the end of the walk.

St James' Park

ROUTE – Through a combination of interesting streets and pleasant parkland, passing three art galleries and a noted Victorian cemetery

TERRAIN – On pavements and surfaced paths with one short climb

REFRESHMENTS – Variety of pubs and cafes en route

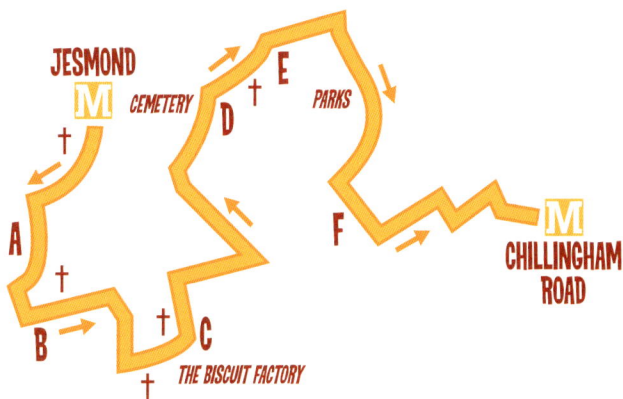

Exit from Jesmond Metro Station, walk ahead for 25 yards and turn right to follow the sign "Jesmond Road (West)". Follow the path passing, on your right, Jesmond Parish Church (1861) by the noted North-East architect, John Dobson. Continue under the flyover to Windsor Place. At the pillar box, bear left, cross Jesmond Road West, and descend towards Northumbria University. At the junction, turn right and follow the pavement as it makes its way to the pedestrian lights near the Customer Service Centre entrance of the Civic Centre. **A**

Turn left, cross over the road at the lights and turn right. After a few yards, you may wish to take the path off to the left to visit the University Gallery which is open to the public. Otherwise continue on the main path to the junction at the NatWest Bank. Turn left and continue ahead to the crossroads, passing the City Hall and its Concert Bar on your right. Diagonally opposite is Burt Hall, named after Thomas Burt, a miner, elected to Parliament in 1873 as one of the first working class MPs. It is topped by the statue of a miner and was formerly the headquarters of the Northumberland Miners' Association. The building is now owned by Northumbria University, as are most of the properties on the section of Northumberland Road along which you are going to walk. On your left, high in the wall, in a niche, is a statue of Dame Allen, founder of the school bearing her name now located in Fenham. **B**

Turn left and walk ahead, passing St James's Church (1822-4) on your left and noting the sculpture of books outside the Ellison Building on your right. At the end of the road bear right to cross the pedestrian bridge over the Central Motorway. Go down the ramp, turn right to cross over the access road, turn left and continue ahead following the pavement as it bears right past Glenamara House. Proceed along Falconar Street, with a stone wall on your right and a pleasant terrace of houses on your left, until you reach the junction. Proceed ahead to cross the road with care. On your right is The Art Works studio and gallery. To continue the walk turn left. Walk ahead past Christ Church (1861), the adjacent primary school and the Queen's Arms. Continue in the same direction down Copland Terrace. You pass the Martin-Luther-Kirche on your left just before arriving at a junction. Bear left and descend to a mini-roundabout and a ring road (B1600-Stoddart Street). Cross over the busy road with care. On your right and well worth visiting is The Biscuit Factory, housing an art gallery and restaurant. **C**

To continue on the walk, turn left (or turn right if exiting from The Biscuit Factory) and continue ahead until your reach some pedestrian lights. Turn right onto the pedestrian path and cycleway and follow it across the green area, ignoring paths off, until you reach a road (Newington Road). Cross over the road, turn left and proceed to the pedestrian lights ahead at Warwick Street. Go across the road and continue in the same direction as the road climbs gradually to Starbeck Avenue with its Sapori cafe and a choice of sandwich bars. Proceed to the T-junction and turn right onto Sandyford Road. Walk ahead with the walls of Jesmond Old Cemetery on your left. Designed by John Dobson, it is said to be one of his finest works. (Opposite Goldspink Lane, you can walk through the gateway across to the imposing north entrance of the cemetery. In addition to Dobson's own grave, it contains the graves of many prominent local Victorian families). To continue on the walk, proceed in the same direction past the entrance to Central Newcastle High School Junior Department, once the house of Dr Gibbs of the song *The Blaydon Races* and later a residential home run by the Sisters of Nazareth. In a short distance, bear right as Sandyford Road converges with Jesmond Road. **D**

Continue along the pavement, passing The Punch Bowl on the opposite side of the road, and just after Roseberry Crescent, at the pedestrian lights, cross over the road to the Pizzeria Santana and turn right. Now proceed ahead past The Cradlewell pub and a parade of shops and Cafe Bar One. Take care as you cross over Osborne Avenue and Shortridge Terrace. On your right you pass Holy Trinity Church (started in 1908 and completed as a war memorial in 1920-2). A few yards beyond the church, bear right and cross, with care, to Jesmond Dene Road. Don't follow the road down but bear left to go across the fine bridge (built by Lord Armstrong's company in 1876-8 and bearing his name) that spans Jesmond Dene and the Ouseburn. **E**

Walk across the bridge, the site of a popular arts and crafts market on Sundays, taking time to admire the excellent views. A few yards beyond the far end of the bridge, turn right to cross another bridge and enter Armstrong Park. Follow the broad path between the trees until eventually you reach an access road. Cross the road with care and continue ahead into Heaton Park. An information board on your right provides some historical details. Continue ahead for a couple of hundred yards, past the ornate pavilion and bowling green on your right, until you reach a crescent with seats on your left and a children's play area over to the right. Leave the broad path to turn left and climb steeply out of the park to Heaton Park View. **F**

Cross over the road, with care, and continue along Stannington Grove to the second road on your left (Cardigan Terrace). Turn left and walk to the crossroads. Cross over the busy road (Heaton Road) at the traffic lights and proceed directly ahead to a T-junction. Turn right and walk a short distance before turning left up Third Avenue. On your right, on the wall of no. 44 you pass a blue plaque, one of a number in the city recognising noted former residents. At the T-junction, with The Chillingham pub on your right, cross with care over the busy road (Chillingham Road), turn right and go over the pedestrian bridge. Turn left and walk the short distance to Chillingham Road Metro Station and the end of the walk.

**St James to Manors
(2.5 miles)**

ROUTE - Follows the line of parts of Newcastle's medieval town wall, through some of the lonelier parts of central Newcastle. Several important historical sites are passed, including three of the four old parish churches which lie inside the wall's boundary

TERRAIN - Mostly on the level. However, in order to appreciate the route of the town wall, there are some very steep ascents and descents via steps

REFRESHMENTS - A wide variety of possibilities throughout the walk

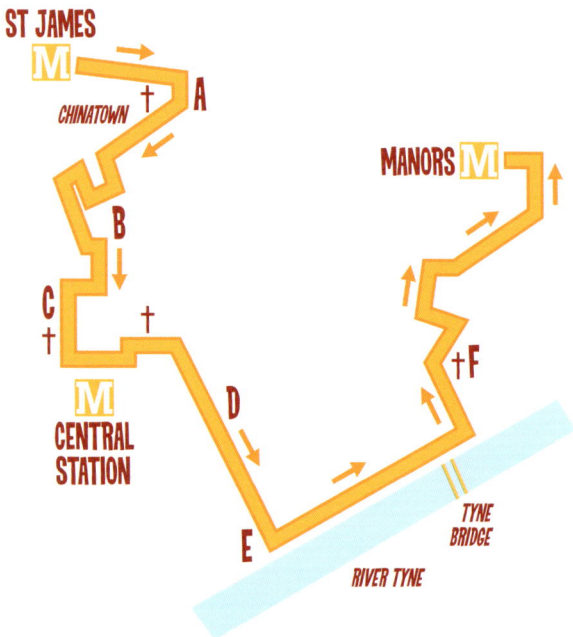

Newcastle gained its name from the "new castle" built in 1080 by Robert Curthose, son of William I. This was basically a strong wooden tower erected on a man-made earthen mount. It was replaced, 100 years later, by Henry II who built a massive stone keep with a surrounding wall. Although there is virtually no trace of the wall, we can still admire the keep, more than 800 years since its original construction. The building of a separate town wall commenced in the 13th century, within 100 years of the completion of Henry II's castle. As a result of the building and subsequent strengthening of the town wall, the defensive wall round the castle keep was, in effect, redundant. When completed, the town wall was two miles long and included seven gates and a series of nineteen strong, semicircular towers interspersed by lookout turrets. The sections of the wall which still exist, and which feature in this walk, give a good idea of the impressive defences possessed by Newcastle in medieval times.

As you pass through the station concourse, notice the posters of Newcastle United stars by Bob Olley. Exit from St James Metro station, bear right and walk past the car park on your right to join a road (Gallowgate). Turn left and walk to the second set of traffic lights. Turn right to cross the road and walk to the ancient parish church of St Andrew. The origins of the present building date from the 12th century and it is generally recognised as the oldest of the city's churches. **A**

Turn right, at the second gate, into the church grounds. Walk to the left of the building past the main entrance. Beyond the church, on your right are two sections of the town wall. Retrace your steps to exit the church grounds and turn right. Walk a few yards and turn right to go up St Andrew's Street (formerly Darn Crook). At the junction turn left into Stowell Street, Newcastle's Chinatown. Walk ahead and, opposite the Shangri-la restaurant - just before No 41, Norden House, go through the archway on the left to Blackfriars and its monastic remains. Walk ahead, then take the last path on the right onto the paved area leading to the buildings and two information panels which give a historical summary and details of recent renovations. **B**

Exit through the arch, past a café/bar, and turn right. Proceed ahead. Cross Stowell Street to an information panel which gives details of the nearby town wall. Go through the opening in the wall. From here you have a good view of this section. The stone-built three storey building ahead is the former fever hospital (1808). Turn left and proceed round the tower remains, then cross Stowell Street and continue ahead on the path, with the town wall on your left. At the end of the road, cross by the traffic lights to the Tyne Theatre and Opera House (originally a theatre, then for some years a cinema before being returned to its original use). Turn left and walk a short distance, then turn second right into the pedestrian section of Pink Lane. Proceed to the junction with Clayton Street. Turn right, walk to the traffic lights and cross over to Bewick Street.

On the right is the Roman Catholic Cathedral Church of St Mary (Pugin 1842-4 – the spire was added in 1872); its Cloister Café is open to the public. **C**

Walk down Bewick Street. At the bottom you can admire the statue of Cardinal Basil Hume (Nigel Boonham 2002). Opposite is the railway station with its splendid portico (John Dobson 1846-50). Turn left, walk past the Thistle Hotel, then turn left into Grainger Street. Proceed to the crossroads. Turn right to cross the road at the lights. On the opposite side of the road is St John the Baptist's Church. The tower is 15th century but the building's origins are much earlier. The walk continues by proceeding ahead on the pavement past the Long Bar on your right. At a stone pillar (with an explanatory plaque below), turn right and walk a few yards to the traffic lights. Cross to an island with the monument to George Stephenson (1862), the noted railway engineer, by the distinguished sculptor John Lough (1798-1876). Turn immediately right and cross by the traffic lights. Turn left and walk a few yards to turn into Orchard Street. Proceed ahead through the tunnel to arrive at a crossroads near The Telegraph pub. On the right is Central Square, an award – winning refurbishment of the former Post Office sorting office. The sculpture *Vulcan* (the blacksmith of the gods) is by Sir Eduardo Paolozzi (2000). Cross over to The Telegraph pub. Walk along the pavement, with the pub on your right, to a well-preserved section of the town wall, beyond which is an information board. **D**

To continue the walk, take the path to the right of the wall and proceed ahead with the wall on your left. (In a gap between buildings over to the right notice the sculpture *Reaching for the Stars* by Kenneth Armitage (2002)). At the end of the path turn right then immediately left and go down steps to arrive at a narrow road (Hanover Street). The granite insets in the road surface were to accommodate the wheels of horse-drawn vehicles. Cross the road and go down the steps straight ahead of you. Keep to the steps on the right. As you descend you can appreciate why the section of the wall which ran over to your right was known as "the breakneck steps"! The steps exit onto a pavement opposite the Copthorne Hotel. A plaque on your right indicates that you are now at the site of the Close Gate. **E**

Turn left and carry straight on. You pass the impressive 500 years old building with high curved exposed beams, now occupied by The Cooperage pub. A little further on, you come to a group of 16th and 17th-century merchants' houses including Bessie Surtees House. This in the care of English Heritage and has an interesting museum (open Monday-Friday, admission free). At the junction, cross the road with extreme care, turn right then left to go under the Tyne Bridge. Proceed ahead, cross Lombard Street, and shortly, turn left at a sign indicating the direction for All Saints Church. Walk ahead to go up some steps. At the top, bear right to walk a short distance up Pilgrim Street and enter the grounds of the former parish church of All Saints (1796). **F**

An information panel on the left provides interesting details. As well as being a venue for concerts and other events, the building is used for worship by an independent church (which calls the building "The Church of St Willibrord with All Saints"). Bear left to exit the church grounds. Turn sharp right and walk down the side of a modern office block for about 30 yards. Turn right up a short flight of steps then turn left. Go down the wide, cobbled steps - take care, they can be slippery. At the bottom, turn left and walk for about 50 yards, then cross the road to go up Croft Stairs. At the top, there is another section of the town wall and the remains of the unusual corner tower, built when the wall was extended to embrace a new area. Exit onto City road. Cross at the pedestrian crossing on your right. Bear right, cross the road and turn right to walk up Melbourne Street to the second crossroads. (At the end of the street on your right is the medieval Sallyport Tower). Turn left and walk ahead. Before you reach the traffic lights, turn left into the business park area and proceed to Manors Metro Station and the end of the walk.

Stowell Street

St James to Fenham to St James (5 miles)

- ↗ **ROUTE** – Through some of Newcastle's attractive parkland and paths to Fenham and return to St James

- 🏃 **TERRAIN** – Mostly on the level on surfaced paths and pavements. There is an optional steep climb over grassland to a viewpoint

- ☕ **REFRESHMENTS** – Three pubs on the route

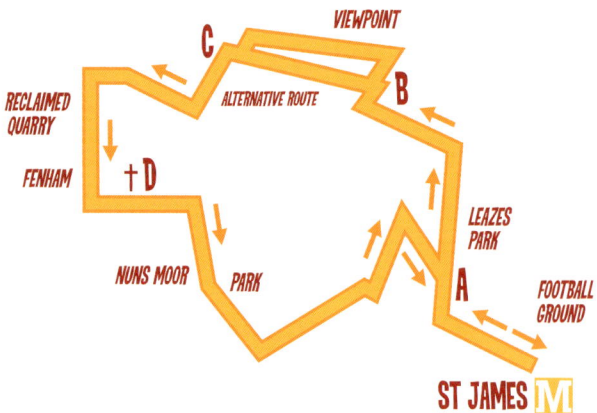

Leave St James Metro Station, turn right and walk alongside the station building. Pass steps on your right (signposted "Football Stadium") and go up the ramp to come to a pavement. Turn right and walk ahead to traffic lights. Carry straight on, across the road, and proceed ahead passing St James' Park football stadium and car park on your right. After 200 yards, opposite The Black Bull pub, turn right onto the broad path. (A plaque on the corner of The Black Bull gives information about Alec Burns (1907-2003), a champion athlete from Elswick Harriers). Proceed up the path to the Jubilee Gates entrance to Leazes Park on your right. You might like to take the opportunity to explore Newcastle's oldest public park, which has recently been restored to its Victorian splendour. **A**

To continue on the walk, don't go through the gates but proceed ahead on the path, with the park wall on your right, to meet a busy road (Richardson Road). Turn left and walk ahead. You pass the Belle Grove Hotel on the left and, on the right in Cross Morpeth Street, the Village Chippy and the Village Stores. At the traffic lights, turn right, cross Richardson Road and walk to the T-junction with Claremont Road. **B**

(The next section includes a fairly steep climb over grassland and can be muddy. If you wish to avoid this, turn left, cross the road with care and proceed to the top of Claremont Road. Keep in the same direction by using the pedestrian lights to cross the busy road and turn left to arrive at a gate **C**).

To continue the walk cross Claremont Road, using the traffic island on your right. Turn left and walk past the bench then go up the ramp to cross the bridge over the dual carriageway. You are about to go onto the Town Moor; its dual ownership (the Council own the land and the Freemen the grazing rights) has contributed to its continuation as an area where citizens can enjoy its vast open space. Descend to go through a gate. After 100 yards or so, turn left to leave the metalled path and join the well-defined path over the grassland, with trees over to your left. Follow this to the top of the hill. At the summit keep to the path as it descends and then climbs to reach the high point, one of the highest in Newcastle. From here you can enjoy panoramic views. In the winter the steep sides provide convenient sledge and ski slopes for local children (and parents!). Keep in the same direction to go down the hill and through a gate. Take the path ahead between the trees and exit near a busy road intersection. Turn left and walk to the pedestrian lights. Cross the road and carry on to cross the bridge over the dual carriageway. Cross the next road, again at pedestrian lights, and after just a few yards, turn right to cross the main road to join the footpath on the other side. Turn left and walk to a gate. **C**

Proceed ahead along the tree-lined path. At the T-junction turn right and walk ahead. Shortly after going through a gate the path runs alongside a busy main road. Carry on and, immediately after the entrance to a subway, take the footpath on the left and follow this through pleasant parkland, reclaimed from a former quarry, to exit at a road. Walk ahead along Kingsway using the pavement on the left-hand side. At the crossroads, turn left and walk ahead. This road is Fenham Hall Drive, which derives its name from Fenham Hall (1745) whose owners included the grandparents of Elizabeth Barrett Browning. After a parade of shops you arrive at the church of St James and St Basil (1931), financed by Sir James Knott, local industrialist and benefactor, in memory of his two sons killed in the First World War. The last stained glass window, just before the crossroads, depicts James and Basil Knott in their soldiers' uniforms. **D**

At the traffic lights go straight ahead, across Wingrove Road North, then turn immediately right to cross Fenham Hall Drive. Turn left and proceed ahead. About 100 yards before the road end, take the public footpath on your right. Follow this across the field and go through the park (Nuns Moor Park). Exit onto a road. Use the traffic lights to cross the road to carry on in the same direction, still in Nuns Moor Park. At a junction of paths continue ahead over the grass to come to a public footpath fingerpost. Take the second path, which goes off to the right, and follow this, passing some trees on your right, to come to a main road (Barrack Road). Turn right and proceed to the pedestrian lights, cross the road and go into Holland Drive. The entrance to the Leazes Inn is along the road to the right. Walk along Holland Drive, using the pavement on the right-hand side. Where the road bears left, carry straight on between the metal barriers to a road. Carry on to a junction and bear right to go through a gate and along the footpath. At a crossing of paths, turn right and proceed ahead to arrive at the Jubilee Gates entrance to Leazes Park. **A**

Don't go through the gates but continue ahead down the broad path. At the end, turn left and retrace your steps, past the football ground, to St James Metro Station and the end of the walk.

The numbers represent the order in which the walks appear in this book; S indicates starting from; F indicates finishes at; S/F indicates starts and finishes from same station